# AMERICA
## I · N · V · A · D · E · S

# AMERICA

## I ★ N ★ V ★ A ★ D ★ E ★ S

**PADDY GRIFFITH**

MALLARD PRESS

**Photography**
UPI/Bettmann
National Archives, Washington, D.C.
Library of Congress
SIPA Press
Keystone Collection
N.A.S.A.

**Editor**
David Gibbon

**Research**
Leora Kahn
Meredith Greenfield

**Commissioning**
Andrew Preston
Laura Potts

**Production**
Ruth Arthur
David Proffit
Sally Connolly

**Design**
Stonecastle Graphics Ltd

**Map Artwork**
Richard Hawke

MALLARD PRESS

An imprint of BDD Promotional Book Company, Inc.,
666 Fifth Avenue, New York, N.Y. 10103.

Mallard Press and its accompanying design and logo are
the trademarks of BDD Promotional Book Company, Inc.

CLB 2345
© 1991 Archive Publishing,
a division of Colour Library Books Ltd.,
Godalming, Surrey, England.
First published in the United States of America
in 1991 by The Mallard Press
Printed and bound in Singapore by Tien Wah Press
All rights reserved
ISBN 0 7924 5377 8

# CONTENTS

# CHAPTER ONE

# AMERICA INVADES!

During the twentieth century America's military operations have taken the form of offensives far more often than defensives. This has not been an accident since, unlike the major nations of continental Europe, the USA has not had to live with the threat of invasion by heavily armed neighbors. At least until the launch of the first Sputnik in 1957, she had been able to bask in the warmth of "free security" at home, allowing her to go to war only "at a time and a place of her own choosing." In other words, America has long enjoyed the invaluable advantage that she can afford to carry her wars into the enemy's territory in a way many other nations cannot. Great natural and industrial resources have further reinforced these advantages to the point where, sometime around 1942, the USA became the dominant global power. It is surely something less than an accident that the Pentagon building in Washington, D.C. – such a famous symbol of worldwide military strength – was first opened that very year.

*General George Crook, scourge of the Plains Indians, with his two Apache scouts and his mule named – somewhat tactlessly – Apache. In military terms, the ease of Crook's victories showed that America enjoyed relatively "free security" at home.*

*The impressive US victory parade held in Paris, France, on 6th October 1944 to mark the liberation of the city. Coming just four months after the D-Day landings, this symbolizes the type of short but triumphant campaign that the American people have come to expect.*

The American taste for offensive military action seems to reflect a certain impatience inherent in the national character. In prolonged defensive operations, such as the war in Vietnam, the troops begin to feel frustrated and the public at home soon runs out of patience. They want to see tangible results in the form of winners, heroes, trophies, toppled enemy dictators and captured enemy capital cities, and all preferably within a single presidential term.

No war that runs through a presidential election will be favourably viewed unless it is obviously already winding down satisfactorily to the sort of conclusion that the public expects. Because neither Korea in 1952 nor Vietnam in 1968 seemed to have been won by the time of the presidential elections, both of these two wars led to the toppling of a Democratic president and the inauguration of a Republican one. Something comparable also seemed to happen in 1920 at the end of WWI, although in that case the issue was no longer the outcome of the war but the nature of the peace treaty – and President Woodrow Wilson had lost his personal control of events due to illness. During the brief period of the war itself the public had actually held firm behind him.

To set against these examples of "public impatience" with American wars, we have some opposite cases of wars that were fought to a finish under unchanged leadership, because they were perceived as victorious crusades. In 1864, towards the end of the Civil War, Lincoln's reelection demonstrated public confidence in his achievements; and in 1944 Franklin D. Roosevelt's fourth term was secured by his successful record as leader and statesman throughout WWII. Nor should we forget that in 1982 Richard M. Nixon was enthusiastically reaffirmed as President because he seemed to be bringing the boys home smoothly from Vietnam, covered by a successful program of "Vietnamization." Watergate would be a postwar trauma for the nation, not a part of the war itself.

The Mexican invasion of 1846-7 is probably the best model of how Americans would like all their wars to be. It was a short, sharp but mobile campaign in which an enemy regime, perceived as corrupt and threatening to democratic aspirations (in this case in Texas), was humbled. Relatively small US spearheads, including a good proportion of citizen-soldiers who had joined up only for the duration, successfully marched on Mexico city and stormed it. As a result of this rapid and relatively cheap victory, the USA won huge territorial benefits, including annexation of most of her present Pacific seaboard. In return for the judicious "investment" of just 1,733 killed in action and some 11,550 who died from other causes, Uncle Sam was able to take over what would soon become one of the richest and sunniest

LEFT

*President Woodrow Wilson comes home in July 1919 after his remarkable molding of European affairs at the Versailles peace conference. Tragically he was unable to cement American solidarity behind the League of Nations, with the result that collective security – and world peace – would prove to be very short lived.*

BELOW

*President Franklin D. Roosevelt owed his third re-election in 1944 to his confident success as a war leader. Here he is photographed with his Pacific Theater commanders, General Douglas MacArthur and Admiral Chester W. Nimitz, shortly before the election.*

LEFT

*The glare of publicity is turned on the Watergate hearings during the summer of 1973, as President Richard M. Nixon is impeached for taking illegal and unconstitutional "short cuts." Although South Vietnam was still undefeated and the USA had successfully withdrawn from the war, there had been no glorious victory and the public mood remained deeply troubled.*

BELOW

*Draftees reporting for military service in 1917. Despite the massive casualties then being suffered by the European armies, these men seem confident of a quick victory. They do not appear to have any sense that the war might turn sour for America.*

of all his states – California. This startling achievement was contrasted in the minds of contemporaries with the the Second Seminole War that started in 1835. In that conflict there were comparable figures of some 1,392 Regular Army killed in action – plus an unknown (but large) number of militia and regulars who died of disease – yet this was a war that settled very little and dragged on for seven weary years.

In 1898 the "lightning war" concept would be applied again, this time against Spain. Influenced by the writings of Alfred Thayer Mahan, son of the celebrated West Point professor Dennis Hart Mahan, many Americans now believed their nation's destiny was to become a great international naval power as well as a continental land power. The fleet stood ready to help the Army win overseas campaigns, and in the event the liberation of Cuba and the Philippines was completed briskly within about three and six months respectively, for the loss of just 290 American soldiers killed in action. Once again there were far more – 2565 – who died of disease. Nevertheless, the cost of winning these two desirable colonial territories must surely be considered "light." It can be contrasted with the Boer War a year later, which cost 22,000 British lives and took two and a half years to complete.

If plentiful political benefits may be won by the offensive form of war, it has also long been

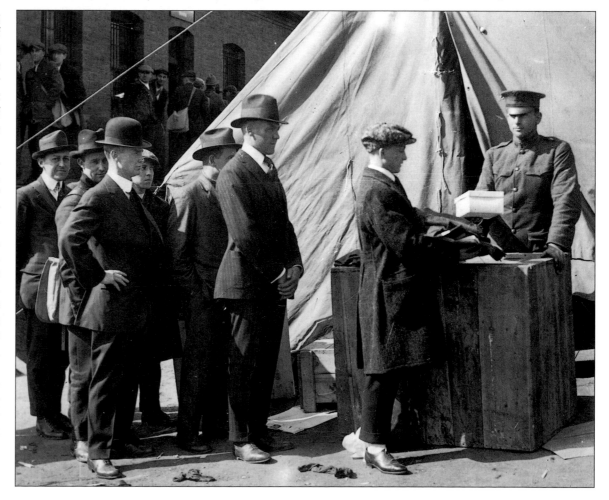

recognized that many purely military advantages may be gained by the same means. Throughout history US military doctrine has usually stressed offensive warfare and maneuvers rather than "mud digging" in static fortifications. The immobile defensive has been deliberately preferred on only a few occasions, when special circumstances applied. This was true for Andrew Jackson's shaky militias at New Orleans in 1815, for example, when he faced an apparently very superior British force. The widespread use of fortifications returned to fashion in the Civil War, when the West Point doctrines of Professor Dennis Hart Mahan seemed for a time to combine with the inexperience of two large militia armies to negate the idea of the offensive altogether. In the twentieth century the defensive has usually been accepted only as an unfortunate temporary pause within general forward thrusts. However, in the trenches along the 38th Parallel in Korea between 1951 and 1953 it took on a novel and different importance. Following the failure of MacArthur's 1950 offensive and the success of the Chinese counter-attack, the establishment of a firm defensive line came to be seen as a diplomatic imperative – the only alternative to a nuclear war. Then in Vietnam the Army reluctantly accepted a generally defensive posture for very much the same reasons, although it still tried to make its low level tactics agile and offensive. "Search and Destroy" came to symbolise all the frustrations of a naturally attacking force held on a leash within South Vietnam, prohibited from hot pursuit into Cambodia, Laos and North Vietnam itself.

More recently a purely defensive posture, relying on high technology firepower, was also preferred by 7th Army in West Germany for a time during the 1970s – but this has now changed back to a much more offensive and mobile concept. The lessons of Vietnam have now been absorbed into the Army's operational Field Manual (designated FM100-5), which since the early 1980s has entirely rejected the idea of reactive, attritional warfare. Instead, it embraces a crushing armored and air-mobile counter-stroke designed to "make the enemy pay." No longer, it is hoped, will American soldiers be able to claim, with Rambo, that "somebody wouldn't let us win."

Perhaps the most important influence on US military thinking in the twentieth century has been the classic Prussian textbook *On War* by Karl von Clausewitz, first published in 1832. During the 1950s and '60s this book inspired a whole generation of nuclear strategists with its central theme that "war is the continuation of politics with the addition of other means." Before that, however, it had already exerted a major influence by its stress on the offensive and the concept of lightning war. Professors at West Point and Fort Leavenworth had long been preaching that mobile operations alone could win positive results, and this became the foundation-stone of US strategy in both World Wars. When Pershing's army entered the fighting on the Western Front in 1918, its aim was to march straight to Berlin, the Kaiser's capital. Initially it had to cope with some defensive fighting at Chateau Thierry, as Ludendorff's spring offensive was finally damped down; but by July it was free to take the war to the enemy, notably in the battles of St. Mihiel and Meuse-Argonne.

Between the wars military theory was led by proponents of offensive warfare – General Adna R. Chaffee and George S. Patton Jr. for armor, and the controversial General Billy Mitchell for air power. When US forces came to Europe in 1942 they initially wanted to land in France and march directly on Hitler's capital – Berlin once again. On this occasion, however, they were dissuaded by their British allies, who after the Dieppe fiasco of August 1942 were only too well aware of the dangers that an assault landing in France might entail. Nevertheless throughout most of the remainder of WWII the Americans continued to argue for a more direct assault on Germany. The British normally tended to be more cautious, apart from a few uncharacteristically reckless episodes such as Montgomery's ill-fated, narrow-fronted thrust to Arnhem in September 1944.

In fact, the main opposition to the offensive idea within the US military has traditionally come neither from cautious allies nor from the concept of the defensive. Instead, it has tended to come

*American wars are not always straightforward or uncontroversial. In this picture Jerry D. Coffin demonstrates his opposition to the Vietnam war by burning his draft card in front of Philadelphia's Independence Hall in October 1967.*

*The bombardment of Vera Cruz at the start of the short but hugely successful Mexican War of 1846-7: a preparatory use of US firepower that may be compared with the air attacks at the start of Operation Desert Storm in January 1991.*

*General Winfield Scott – "Old Fuss and Feathers" as he was affectionately known – enters Mexico City at the moment of triumph. American soldiers have often taken this campaign as a model, believing that true victory in war demands the total defeat of the enemy's army and the capture of his capital city.*

from the concept of "technology" or "firepower." If an expendable shell or bomb can be sent to blow up or otherwise kill the enemy, there will be no need to send an irreplaceable man. As early as the Revolutionary War, propagandists were contrasting the unsubtle massed bayonet assaults of the British and their mercenaries with the more intelligent sniping by individualist Americans using the high-precision Kentucky long rifle. In the Civil War there was also great enthusiasm for new technologies such as land and sea "torpedoes," repeating rifles, and even machine guns – and a corresponding disenchantment with the bayonet. Throughout history, in fact, the USA has been at the forefront of weapon design, and this has never been more true than in the twentieth century. It was she who led the way in the 1940s with such innovations as the self-defending bomber, the self-sufficient carrier task group with a "floating base," and the Manhattan project itself. She is also currently worrying potential enemies with her long-range airborne surveillance, her various families of "Assault Breaker"-type anti-armor top attack rocket systems, and her futuristic electro-magnetic rail gun.

This technological orientation of American military thinking certainly stems partly from the technological orientation of American society as a whole. However, the story does not stop there. The need to multiply numbers by machinery – or to save casualties by firepower – is also a direct result of the way the military profession is viewed by US society.

Firstly, we must remember that throughout history the regular army has almost always been small in peacetime. On the day the Civil War broke out it numbered a mere 14,000 men. On the day of Pearl Harbor, despite massive reinforcement by peacetime conscription over the previous eighteen months, it could field only one combat-ready division. Admittedly the start of the Cold War around 1947 allowed greater force levels to be maintained; but in Germany during the last few decades there have still been only about a third of a million Americans to set against some 1.5 million Soviet troops (or to compare with 0.9 million West Germans). In such circumstances it is not difficult to see how Americans have often been tempted to look for "force multipliers" in the field of superior technology and firepower, rather than of manpower.

Furthermore, unlike many continental European powers America is unaccustomed to making large and tragic human sacrifices on the altar of battle. Nor is the Army traditionally held in any very great esteem during peacetime. The nineteenth century champions of military professionalism – generals such as Winfield Scott, George McClellan and Emory Upton – found themselves heavily outvoted by the more populist supporters of citizen militias and temporary soldiers. The widespread feeling was that "war is far too important to be entrusted to soldiers" – especially since the total subordination of the Army to the elected political authorities is centrally enshrined in the Constitution. Through all its history USA has enjoyed an enviable freedom from military coups, and not even General Douglas MacArthur in 1951, despite his very strong popular support, felt able to make a truly political response to his dismissal by President Truman from overall command in Korea.

If there is to be a war at all, therefore, Americans like it to be a quick, cheap and decisive action by the whole nation: not an endemic condition that maintains a militarist elite in power through a protracted loss of life. If technology can hasten a positive result and minimise US casualties, then technology must be fervently embraced. Career soldiers may have an important role in harnessing the technology to best effect, and advising on its use, but ultimately they remain the servants of broad masses of citizen soldiers whom the technology is designed to spare from heavy losses.

The Constitution permits every citizen to own

a gun; but this was not, as is sometimes incorrectly assumed today, originally intended as a defence against freelance burglars or casual muggers. Instead, the idea was to allow the private citizen to beat off tyrannical rulers and their heavily-armed minions. In 1777 this meant King George and his British redcoats; but in later times it came to stand more for the agents of a central government seeking to erode states' rights or individual freedoms. The Civil War itself started with the forceful eviction of federal troops from South Carolina; while more recently the Watergate episode of 1973 starkly reveals the depth of resentment that can still be mobilised when central government seems to be overstepping its constitutional powers.

Each state's militia – termed "National Guard" since the late nineteenth century army reforms – was always seen as a means of removing expensive and unrepresentative federal troops from police, internal security or counter-insurgency tasks within that state's territory. Indeed, because the USA was originally set up by an anti-colonial revolution, the very concept of "counter-insurgency" has itself been traditionally alien to most of her citizens. The chief exceptions to this rule have been the many Indian campaigns of the nineteenth century – although these were usually perceived as small external expeditions to secure new land and fight mainforce battles, with a crusading belief in the rightness of the cause, rather than as low-level police operations in areas that had already been properly settled.

Even on foreign soil Americans have often found it difficult to grasp the full meaning of "counter-insurgency," or to apply it effectively. Admittedly Uncle Sam has conducted a number of successful internal security campaigns in the twentieth century, ranging from the Philippines in 1899-1906 through Greece in 1947-9. However, as late as Vietnam in the 1960s – and despite much preliminary study – there were still some serious misconceptions. For example the army's main duty was not interpreted as counter-insurgency at all, but as going out in the old way to fight big battles in a "mainforce war." Similarly the Green Berets, who were widely advertised as "counter-insurgency experts," in the event found themselves performing a very different role among the montagnard population of the central highlands. Like the OSS in France during WWII, the Green Berets' task was less to police an area in revolt than to organise popular resistance behind enemy lines – in other words to *create* an insurgency, not stop one. In more recent times, during the post-Vietnam backlash, the very word "counter-insurgency" has been declared taboo. It has been replaced in the technical debate by the more politically neutral phrase "low intensity conflict."

One result of the regular army's traditional exclusion from an internal role within the USA has been a marked tendency, in Robert McNamara's phrase, to "play the accordion with manpower." In peaceful times the professional army has usually been very small indeed by European standards, confining itself to ceremonial duties, technical research and the preservation of specialist expertize. In wartime, by contrast, it has usually had to expand further and faster than is usual for European armies, creating many problems of training, supply and transportation to the theater of war. This feature was present in all the nineteenth century conflicts, but it has reappeared no less obviously in the twentieth. Despite such efforts as Howard Coffin's Industrial Preparedness Committee, from 1913 onwards, in 1918 Pershing's army in France could not be armed with more than a handful of tanks, guns and planes that had been made in the USA. Nor could Eisenhower's army of November 1942 – almost a year after America had entered the war – deploy anything like enough strength to attempt an invasion of Europe. It had to be landed in North Africa, instead.

Immediately after victory in 1945 army numbers again declined sharply; although the start of the Cold War would soon reverse this trend. Even so, the mainforce deployment to Vietnam in 1965 was still dogged by some quite familiar types of unpreparedness, improvisation and logistical delay. Cargo ships often had to wait in line for several months off Saigon Harbor before their turn came to land war stores. Field

LEFT

*One of the earliest war photographs, this daguerreotype shows General Wood and his staff in the streets of occupied Saltillo, near Monterrey, during the 1846 invasion of Mexico.*

RIGHT

*The end of the nineteenth century saw a new imperialism in the USA; an enlarged navy, the conquest of Cuba and the Philippines, and participation in the 1900 international carve-up of China. American troops are here seen stepping confidently into Peking.*

BELOW

*The city of Los Angeles in June 1945 enthusiastically welcomes Army General George S. Patton, Jr. and Air Force General James H. Doolittle – two of America's foremost military heroes in another enormously successful yet still relatively short war.*

commanders also found themselves restricted in the number of troops they could commit to combat – and were usually outnumbered by the enemy. Commentators have often missed the vital importance of such factors in the failure to secure a decisive result between 1965 and 1968: an outcome that might have led to some very different directions in the whole of world history during the 1970s and 1980s.

An important part of the problem of unpreparedness is that, because American wars are usually fought beyond the boundaries of the fifty states, everything has to be transported there by sea or air. In the present book we will be looking mainly at the actions of US ground forces; but in this category we certainly include airborne soldiers and marines. Nor should we forget the vital part played by the Navy and Air Force in every operation. More perhaps than any other nation's forces, American troops and their supplies can expect to arrive in a theater of war by sea or air, supported in combat by naval gunfire and aerial bombardment alike. The Air Force will provide overhead cover and interdiction missions, while the Navy imposes a blockade against enemy lines of supply. All these and many other Air Force and Navy roles make it especially artificial, in American operations, to talk of the "ground forces" as an entity separate from other services.

The "American way of war" has often seemed to be rather different from that of other nations, springing as it does from a unique strategic, technological, social and political background. Americans have certainly been lucky to enjoy a high measure of "free security" at home, but they have also skillfully cashed in on this by their scientific mastery and awesome ability to project power globally. Nevertheless, at the end of the day an "American battle" is really not all that very different from anyone else's, since it still ultimately comes down to the fighting qualities of the individual soldier "with his ass in the grass," and "where the rubber meets the road." At the end of the day everything depends on his ability to keep on doing the right thing even though he is numbed and isolated by the enemy's fire; shocked by the loss of comrades, and exhausted by days of stress and sleeplessness. It must be said that in his twentieth century wars, the American soldier has shown himself no more wanting in these qualities than the soldiers of any other nation.

RIGHT

*West Point was originally founded on the model of Napoleon's École Polytechnique as a school of military science, engineering and especially mathematics. This has sometimes led its alumni to favor firepower and fortification solutions, rather than more traditional miltary doctrines based on maneuver and shock action.*

LEFT

*West Point classes in English and German may have helped to counter-balance the influence of science at the school – and may even have helped officers to read military classics such as* On War, *written by the Prussian General Karl Von Clausewitz.*

RIGHT

*Another counter-measure to science at West Point has always been the school's stress on drill, ceremonial dress and the traditional Honor Code.*

ABOVE

The flamboyant, cigar-smoking General George S. Patton, Jr. attends a tactical briefing in 1944. From 1917 he had been a pioneer of armored warfare, representing an important twinning of the offensive principle with advanced technology as "the American way of war."

LEFT

Some of the West Point class of 1888 – a year in which John J. Pershing was the academy's president, but when Civil War fashions were clearly still influencing the uniforms.

RIGHT

General Adna R. Chaffee, Jr. was the son of a hard-fighting cavalryman who had served from the Civil War through China in 1900. Following very much in his father's footsteps – literally during the Boxer Rising, then symbolically in 1918 France – the younger Chaffee established himself between the world wars as the true architect of the armored forces that would add so much mobility and offensive edge to the US Army in World War Two.

*Even at the height of the Cold War – here an American patrol observes a Berlin border crossing in 1964 – the USA contributed only a relatively small proportion of the manpower defending Germany. Her main contribution lay in nuclear deterrence, air power and technological weaponry.*

*Historically the US Army has usually been small, and manned by volunteers more often than by draftees. Recruiting has normally relied on public relations skills, as exemplified by this folksy timber-frame cabin, offered to the New York public as a tempting alternative to the surrounding cityscape just before World War One.*

*Secretary of War Elihu Root reformed the Army and its staff during the years immediately following the Spanish-American War; but he did not confine himself narrowly to the professional army. Instead, he wished to exploit the potential of the National Guard as a new and much better-prepared form of the popular militias that in past wars had too often been thrown naked into the cauldron of battle.*

ABOVE

President Harry S. Truman meeting the popular and outspoken General Douglas MacArthur at the height of the Korean crisis, Wake Island 15th October 1950. The two leaders could not agree on strategy; but it speaks volumes for the strength of the Constitution that political authority could prevail so easily and smoothly over military power.

RIGHT

A potent factor in modern American war-making is a rapidly increasing dread of heavy casualties. The official 1944 caption for this picture of a Signal Corps victim happily stressed that occupational therapy and technology had soon allowed him to smoke his cigarette "as naturally as ever." If the same photograph had been taken in 1991, however, the caption would surely have been very different.

ABOVE

*Although casualties in the eight-year Vietnam War were actually relatively light by normal military standards, every wheelchair and every body bag made an ineradicable impact on the public consciousness. This picture was taken at an anti-war protest in 1967*

ABOVE

*US Marines in action during the "brushfire"
Nicaraguan campaign of 1912; an early example of
Uncle Sam's readiness to conduct low intensity
warfare within neighboring American states, in
pursuance of the Monroe Doctrine and (for Cuba)
the 1901 Platt Amendment.*

ABOVE

*A rough and ready outdoor Marine camp during the Haiti intervention of 1915.*

LEFT

*Sailiors from USS* Denver *performing embassy guard duties during the temporary occupation of Puerta Cortez, Honduras, in March 1924.*

*US Marines once again in Nicaragua, this time in 1927 with a rather neater camp site and apparently more uniform attire than in their earlier interventions*

*An apparently unwelcome US soldier maintaining the tradition of Caribbean intervention at the height of the so-called "Counter- Insurgency Era," Dominican Republic 1965.*

RIGHT

*Popular approval of the military has often been low in peacetime but high in wartime, especially when a mass army has had to be raised. On this occasion in November 1944 over 80,000 spectators filled Yankee Stadium, New York, to applaud the Army Eleven as they beat the Notre Dame Fighting Irish by 46-0.*

BELOW

*Mass warfare greatly increases popular participation in war industries. Pictured here is a busy Second World War production line set up to provide rubber boats for naval aviators.*

ABOVE

The scene in 1919 at the start of the Army's long journey home from France. America's great physical remoteness from the theaters of operations has led to similarly significant moments in almost all her wars.

RIGHT

A Navy landing craft being loaded in Belgium for transport to the 1945 Rhine crossings. This happened to be the Navy's first major river crossing in Europe, although in many other wars the dictates of strategic geography had already often brought the Army and Navy into exceptionally close co-operation with each other.

One result of America's "free security" is that her troops usually have to make friends in strange foreign lands – in this case Chartres, France, in 1944.

"East or West, home's best"... and so is victory. V-E Day in Times Square, New York 1945.

# CHAPTER TWO

# FROM MEXICO TO THE MEUSE

*Pershing's campaigns, 1916-1918*

The Mexican Revolution of 1910 created a series of political crises within the country, with the government swinging wildly from dictatorship to constitutional democracy, and then back again. For the United States this posed some classic policy dilemmas, modern variants of which have subsequently become a permanent part of the whole Central American scene. In a nutshell, Uncle Sam had to decide between supporting the dictators – who protected American oil interests but were repressive and undemocratic – or supporting the constitutionalists who enjoyed popular support but opposed the *Gringos*.

*American sailors in the streets of Vera Cruz, 1914, during the operation to avenge the arrest of a party of US Marines. Note the Colt-Browning M1895 machine gun, John Browning's first experimental design that would lead to a long line of more successful Browning guns in US service.*

*General John J. "Black Jack" Pershing (right) with Pancho Villa (center) at El Paso, Texas, in 1914. At this time the USA was supporting Villa's role in the Mexican Revolution – but that would soon change.*

At first America backed the dictators; but after Victoriano Huerta's brutal coup in early 1913 President Woodrow Wilson threw in his lot with the constitutionalists. This led to blows in April the following year, when Huerta's men arrested a party of US marines in Tampico. The US Navy then retaliated by seizing Vera Cruz, and Huerta was eventually toppled. These events were followed by a deepening civil war, however, as the constitutional parties themselves fragmented. By 1916 the USA was aligned behind the conservative government of Venustiano Carranza, supporting him against the more radical guerrilla leaders Emiliano Zapata in the south, and Pancho Villa in the north.

It was Villa who posed the biggest threat to US interests, since his followers had been involved in a series of border skirmishes from 1915 onwards. Then in 1916 they raided Columbus, New Mexico, and killed seventeen Americans – which in turn provoked a serious deployment of the US Army. Starting on 15th March, General John J. "Black Jack" Pershing led a punitive expedition of some 12,000 regulars in search of Pancho Villa, while almost 158,000 National Guards were mobilized to protect his rear and the border areas. Given the threatening situation in Europe, this last measure was quickly expanded into a much wider National Defense Act that would activate some 670,000 men within five years – although even this threefold expansion was soon to be completely overtaken by events.

Pershing himself was an expert in the strategy and tactics of "small wars," having fought in several Indian campaigns and against the Spanish in Cuba, 1898, and then against the Moros in the Philippines. In Mexico he led his expedition with flair and gripped it with a firm hand, successfully beating off a number of guerrilla attacks and fully establishing his reputation in the public mind. However, he failed to apprehend Pancho Villa and finally fell back across the border in January 1917.

Pershing was nevertheless the general of the hour, and the natural choice to be Commander in Chief of the American Expeditionary Force (AEF) when war was declared against Germany on 6th April. Indeed, the war itself was provoked partly by German plots to encourage Mexican rebels to invade Texas. When he arrived in France in June, however, Pershing found he had no army worthy of the name. Initially there were only the improvised 1st Infantry Division, amalgamated from many regular units, and the equally polyglot 42nd National Guard "Rainbow" Division. This put him at a distinct disadvantage in dealing with his French and British allies, who had already borne the brunt of unprecedentedly bitter fighting for almost three years before US troops first landed in France – and would continue to do so for a further year. They could not help noticing that,

although the first Americans were killed in the trenches at the start of November 1917, it would be six more months before a major American battle would be fought – on the Marne in June 1918 – and ten months before the long awaited massed attack was mounted, at St. Mihiel just two months before the war finally ended. Whereas 0.8 million British and 1.4 million French would be killed in this conflict, America would suffer 53,402 killed in action (including Navy and Marines) – a figure lower even than the 56,639 endured by the far smaller Canadian forces. Not unnaturally, the Europeans were sometimes sarcastic at this imbalance of sacrifice, and they were just as insistent that Pershing should commit his troops to battle during 1917 as Joseph Stalin would later be for the opening of a second front in 1942.

Apart from pressing ahead with training and equipping his army as quickly as possible, Pershing's response to allied pressure was twofold. In the first place he urgently asked his home government to supply at least a million men by May 1918, with two million more in the longer term. The government's response was to introduce the Selective Draft Act on 5th June 1917, which would eventually produce a total force of no less than four million men, or a third as many again as Pershing had requested. A total of 42 divisions and their supporting services would be deployed to France before the Armistice. Since at this time an American division comprised some 27,000 men, or about twice as many as was normal in European armies, it is clear that Pershing's original targets were more than handsomely met.

Secondly, Pershing spent many long hours with his allies arguing about the manner in which American troops should be commited to battle. He passionately believed they should not be squandered piecemeal or prematurely, as reinforcements for whichever points in the line might happen to be threatened from one moment to the next. Instead, they should be husbanded as a single consolidated *masse de manoeuvre*, and then all be thrown in together to achieve a decisive effect. Pershing distrusted what he saw as his allies' defensive, attrition-orientated (and even defeatist) mentality. He wanted to use his uncorrupted young spearhead of one million American troops for a crushing final offensive: an assault that would break the trench deadlock once and for all, and take the lead in the great advance to Berlin. Only in this way, he reasoned, would the USA win the right to its full share in the ultimate peace negotiations.

These arguments were not in themselves particularly convincing, since the beleaguered Western allies would surely have given full diplomatic recognition to any American manpower assistance, regardless of the particular form in which it was offered. The United States had for long been a central provider of munitions to the alliance, so her overall contribution to the war effort was way beyond question. In fact Pershing's strategy was potentially counter productive, since the European allies could easily represent it as a case of "the USA wanting to fight to the last Frenchman, and then charge in to grab the glory once all the nastiness was over." Nor

could anyone see how the green American troops – unused to modern battle, lacking in higher staffs, and equipped mainly with European weaponry – might possess some novel key that could unlock the trench deadlock to create the successful offensive that had for so long eluded the Europeans. Nor, in the event, did they actually possess such a key. Indeed, on 26th February 1918, one American unit had been so inexperienced in chemical warfare that it suffered no less than 95% casualties in a gas attack that its allies might have considered "routine." At Belleau Wood in June the Marines used precisely the same unsubtle massed frontal assault tactics that had already been notoriously discredited following the British assault on the Somme just two years earlier.

For all this, Pershing was ultimately able to carry his point because of one unquantifiable but vitally important factor. It turned out that merely the arrival of American troops in France was enough, in itself, to create a truly awesome psychological impact on both sides. To the Germans it demonstrated that their own fresh reinforcements, recently released by victory in Russia, could be more than matched by the Western allies. To the French and British, on the other hand, it gave deep reassurance that there was still "something in reserve" behind the front line. That line nearly broke on two occasions; first during the French mutinies of April-June 1917, and then under the shock of Ludendorff's March 1918 offensive. In both cases, especially the second, it was the potential American presence – even without any commitment in combat – that helped give allied leaders the confidence they needed to weather the storm. The Americans, in other words, were able to play the same part as the Prussians at Waterloo. They "kept their sabers in hand" while the two sides fought each other to a standstill; yet all the while they were exercising a vital leverage on the minds of the two protagonists.

Actually US troops did see some combat before Pershing unleashed his main assault in September 1918. Many individual units were exposed to "battle inoculation" during the months preceding the German offensive of March 1918 – usually in the many quiet sectors of the French line, towards the eastern end of the Western Front. Then, when the front line started to give way, Pershing abandoned his earlier policy of "no piecemeal commitment," and accepted that the allies could use US troops in whatever way they wished. At first this did not amount to a very great deal, since so few trained and fully-equipped divisions were available. In front of Amiens at the start of April, during Ludendorff's first drive, no more than a few engineers were available to help out in the firing line. It was only during the third German drive, at the end of May, that sizeable forces could be put in place, under French command.

On 28th May the 1st Division mounted the first American offensive operation of the war, against the village of Cantigny near Montdidier. It was limited in scope, but entirely successful both in seizing ground and in holding it against counter-attacks. Then the 2nd and 3rd Divisions came into action around Chateau Thierry, the closest point to Paris that the Germans would reach in their 1918 offensives. There was stiff – even epic – fighting, during which the Americans held the line in grand style, and inspired their French comrades with a new spirit. At Belleau Wood to the northwest of Chateau Thierry there had been complaints that the retreating French had initially abandoned some US troops in their general haste and demoralisation. During June, however, there was a distinct stiffening of resistance. Nevertheless it fell to the Americans to recapture the commanding Belleau Wood itself, which was achieved only with great difficulty. In

ABOVE RIGHT

*Some of Pancho Villa's raiders from Columbus, New Mexico, after they had eventually been run to ground by Pershing's troops in the Mexican mountains, 1916.*

RIGHT

*Villa (at wheel of the automobile) and his secretary, Trillo, met a violent death at Parral, Chihuahua, on 20th July 1923. Ironically, he had just retired from politics.*

a three week battle the 4th Marine Brigade advanced no more than a mile through a tangle of rocks, trees and interlocking machine gun nests. It sustained almost 6,000 casualties; nearly as many as would later be sustained by the whole 1st Division in the Aisne-Marne offensive – or by four entire Army Corps during the St. Mihiel offensive. Belleau Wood was thus a distinct "Pyrrhic" victory, which perhaps did more to confront Americans with the inner nature of the Western Front than any other event.

Meanwhile, Ludendorff was mounting his fourth and fifth spring offensives on either side of Pershing's "center of gravity" at Chateau Thierry, albeit with ever-decreasing forces. On 8th June he targeted the sector between Montdidier and Soissons, but achieved no surprise and made little progress. By the 11th the Americans and French were already launching counter-attacks, and the line was held. Then in mid-July the Germans struck out on either side of Reims, to the east of Chateau Thierry, although once again they made little headway. The 38th Infantry Regiment of the US 3rd Division particularly distinguished itself in a defensive battle fought under unpromising circumstances, once again holding the line of the river Marne.

The action now became fast and furious. On 18th July, just one day after Ludendorff had finally expended his offensive impetus, the allies seized the initiative in this sector by unleashing their Aisne-Marne offensive. In fact this operation should more properly have been termed the "Marne-Vesle" offensive, since it started at

ABOVE

*Germany's U-boat campaign did much to bring the USA into the war in 1917, not least the sinking of the British liner* Lusitania *on 7th May 1915. One hundred twenty-eight American passengers perished in the attack – but Britain tried to conceal the fact that the ship was also carrying ordnance stores and could thus be seen as a legitimate target. The notice shown here was a "fair warning" issued on 22nd April by the German embassy in Washington, D.C.*

LEFT

*American tourists caught in Europe at the outbreak of the First World War sail home on USS Cincinnati.*

Chateau Thierry on the Marne and stopped on 6th August along the line of the river Vesle, a few miles short of the Aisne. However that may be, the attack suffered initial setbacks and heavy casualties, but was ultimately a complete success and marked an important turning point in allied fortunes. This operation demonstrated firstly that the Germans were demoralized by a combination of battlefield failures, short rations and Spanish influenza. They were "on the run" and could be levered out of their positions provided rational tactics were used. Second, despite some very primitive Moroccan infantry charging, and at least one tragic French cavalry attack, this offensive represented a major exploitation of technology on the allied side. General Mangin, "the butcher of Verdun," with his American allies well to the fore, rolled forward with a good mixture of all arms – not just artillery and infantry, but especially tanks and aircraft. Finally, the Aisne-Marne offensive showed major American formations in action for the very first time, even though they were not yet coordinated as a single American Expeditionary Force (AEF).

No less than eight US divisions – equivalent to sixteen allied divisions – took some part in the attack, and accounted for approximately one sixth of its overall frontage and area. These formations still remained subordinate to higher French direction, under three separate army HQs, but on this occasion French staffwork was found to be fully equal to the demands placed upon it. The green American troops were successfully leap-frogged through the various stages of the operation, being relieved and taken out of the line where necessary, and supported by friendly units on each flank. In this way they were able to play a useful part in a combined allied operation, even though they still showed some tactical naïveté, and were not yet ready to mount an independent battle on their own behalf. In preparation for this impending next stage, however, a US First Army headquarters was formally set up on 24th July.

Pershing had to wait six weeks before all his assets could be consolidated under his own hand for the first truly "American" attack. This had originally been intended entirely for the St. Mihiel salient; but the quickening pace of the war meant that its main axis soon had to be shifted to the north and west, aiming through the Argonne forest towards the key rail junction at Mézières. Nevertheless, a reduced version of the original St. Mihiel attack was still launched on 12th September, with over a quarter of a million Americans attacking together, supported by five French divisions that were this time under US command. Firepower came from 2,971 guns, 276 tanks and an unprecedented mass of 1,500 aircraft. Despite very strong terrain and enemy fortifications, logistic chaos and a complete lack of surprise,

progress was unexpectedly rapid. Most of the fifteen-mile deep salient was cleared in less than two days.

This apparently dramatic success may be attributed in part to the enthusiasm and strength of the attackers; but it was also partly due to the fortunate coincidence that the Germans were starting to withdraw to a shorter line at the precise moment the attack was launched. They scarcely fought back at all, except with light rearguards; nor did Pershing go on to try to bounce them out of their fallback position on the far side of the salient. The chance was missed to press on to the Germans' fortified strategic pivot at Metz. Indeed, some cynics even suggested the Americans had merely conducted a relief of sentries in the St. Mihiel lines. They did nevertheless capture over 15,000 of the enemy and some 257 guns, as against just 7,000 US casualties. Pershing's young army – the so-called "thin green line" – also won some great psychological benefits from the battle, which helped cement both its self-confidence and its cohesion for the still grimmer battle that was yet to come.

September 26th was the day appointed for the start of the Meuse-Argonne offensive, intended to thrust north towards Mézières through unpromisingly close country along the left flank of the old Verdun battlefield. In successive days the American action would be joined by other allied attacks all along the Western Front, reaching a grand crescendo by the start of October. As a general plan, this amounted to an exercise in straightforward attrition: scarcely a subtle response to the increased power of modern

defences. However, it did represent a timely intensification of pressure against the Germans at a moment when their army was still reeling from the defeats of summer, and their civilian population was facing a cruel winter of destitution and famine.

Unfortunately for the Americans, however, their own particular part in the general plan had been hastily improvised, so they could not at first call upon the seasoned veterans of St. Mihiel. Nor did the Germans oblige by immediately withdrawing, as they had in the earlier battle, since they fully understood the vital strategic importance of the Mézières rail center they were defending. Raw US regiments therefore found themselves being thrown into a much larger and more menacing version of Belleau Wood, facing strong opposition but lacking the full range of training and equipment that was needed. Despite such military epics as the "lost battalion" of the 77th Division, which held out for five days surrounded by the enemy, and Tennessee Corporal Alvin C. York's personal killing or capturing of 147 Germans, the battle degenerated inexorably into attritional infantry combat. Progress was disappointingly slow, and the imposing Kriemhilde position would not be breached until five long weeks of bitter fighting had been completed.

Actually the Americans did enjoy the advantages of surprise, with an initial numerical superiority of around eight to one in men along a 24 mile frontage, supported by some 4,000 guns – 1,000 more than at St. Mihiel. Altogether some 1.2 million Americans would eventually become

FAR LEFT

*A female recruiter for the US Marine Corps distributing literature in Boston, Massachusetts, March 1917.*

LEFT

*The traditional scene as a country family sends a son to war.*

BELOW

*Physical examination of draftees in New York, 1917. European allies were universally impressed by what they perceived as the large size of American soldiers.*

involved in this battle, or something like 50,000 per mile of front. However, they could call upon only 820 aircraft and 189 tanks – significantly fewer in both cases than for the easier St. Mihiel battle. These totals would in any case be rapidly reduced by the wear and tear of combat. Thus, after ten days only eighteen tanks were still running, and their legendary leader, Colonel George S. Patton Jr., had been wounded. As the fighting line advanced northwards, furthermore, the aircraft found themselves over extended and too far from their bases for a long loiter over the battlefield. And meanwhile the enemy kept on winning the time he needed to reinforce his key positions.

Apart from German resistance, the most difficult feature of the Meuse-Argonne fighting lay in the field of logistics. The initial approach march had been a great success, masterminded by Colonel George C. Marshall. Then, when the initial assault lost impetus by the beginning of October, there was a complex but equally successful substitution of veteran formations for the green troops who had opened the battle.

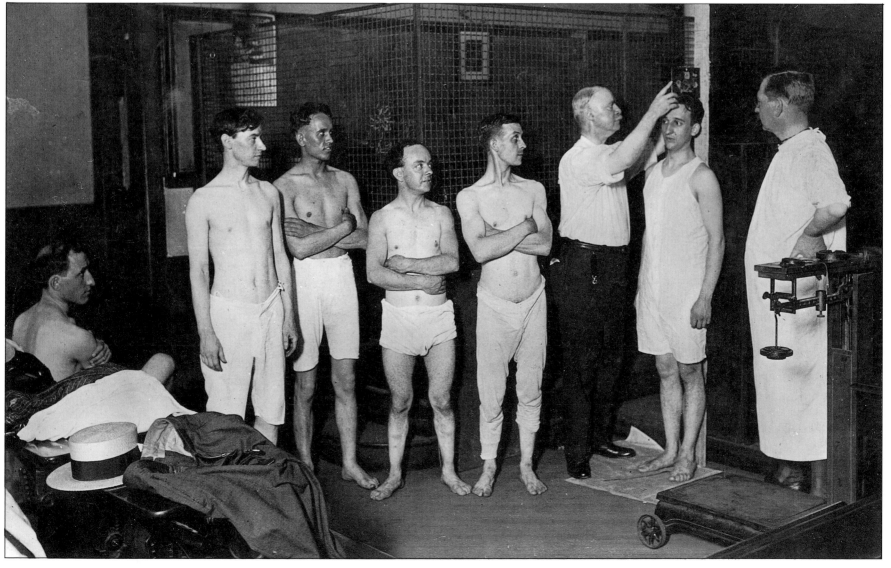

However, the supply arrangements quickly broke down under the combination of poor roads and inexperienced junior staff officers. Paradoxically, it was the very numerical superiority of the Americans that most contributed to the congestion. Units were too closely packed together. They lost their way or became separated either from their replenishment echelons or from their guns. Their attacking impetus was blunted as the weather worsened and the front was extended to include the notorious Heights of the Meuse, directly north from Verdun itself, which had been a major German stronghold for almost three years.

It was only from 1st November that movement was restored to the Meuse-Argonne front, partly through a radical reorganization of the artillery within the spearhead V Corps. Whereas it had previously taken 35 days to advance ten miles, it now took the last eleven days of the war to advance more than twenty miles – marking an acceleration of around six times the previous rate. The gloomy Argonne forest was left far behind. Buzancy fell, and Sedan was finally reached – although in deference to memories of 1870 its ultimate capture was conceded to the vengeful French. What an irony it was that the pendulum of history would return to this same spot for a third time, in the spring of 1940, when Guderian's *Panzers* broke loose there for the victorious rampage towards Dunkirk!

Overall, the Meuse-Argonne battle cost some 120,000 US casualties – or something more than a third of all those suffered in the war. It was as grisly an affair as many of the earlier British and French offensives, fought when those armies were at a similarly fresh point on the lethal "learning curve" of combat by which soldiers must live or die. Unlike some of those earlier offensives, however, the Meuse-Argonne was at least crowned with ultimate victory. Even though the Germans on this sector were never broken and were able to make an orderly retreat, they were forced back more than thirty miles from ground

of their own choosing, and did eventually lose their vital rail link through Mézières.

The Germans also committed some 47 divisions in the course of the battle, which was a very major proportion of their total fighting strength – perhaps as much as a fifth or even a quarter. If British and French commentators have tended to be dismissive of US efforts on this sector, therefore, the Americans have every right to reply that they successfully pinned down a very greatly disproportionate number of the enemy. It is interesting to note that in 1944 in Normandy the boot would be very firmly on the other foot, when Montgomery's attritional British offensives made little headway and evoked the generalized scorn of the American press. Like Pershing in 1918, however, his taut reply was simply that he had drawn off sufficient German reserves to allow a more decisive attack to be launched by his allies

## THE WESTERN FRONT, 1918

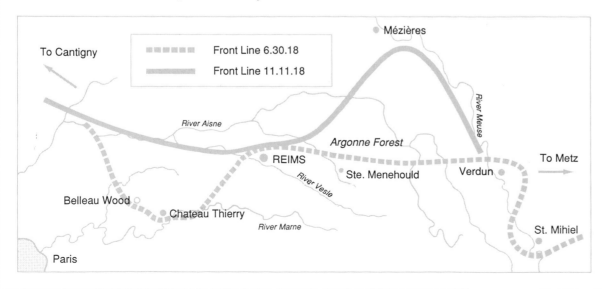

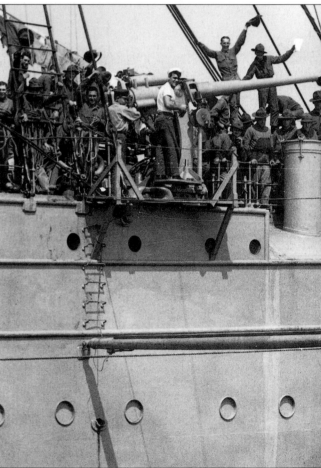

elsewhere. (The question of whether or not this amounted to true military genius must be left to others to decide).

The First World War marked a brutal and disillusioning turning point in the annals of the American military. Whereas it had previously conducted its business on a very small and "colonial" scale – apart from the Civil War itself – it now found itself confronted by the harsh realities of mass warfare in the deep industrial era. Despite

LEFT

*"Marinettes" take the oath to serve the USA in 1917, although women were not authorized to become permanent regular members of the Marine Corps until 1948.*

RIGHT

*US and French troops set out to raid the Mecklenburg trench, Badonviller, in March 1918. At this time the Americans were still operating only in small units closely co-operating with allied troops, in the interests of "combat innoculation." The use of British steel helmets – as well as much British and French heavy weaponry – testifies how the speed and scale of US mobilization outstripped industrial preparedness.*

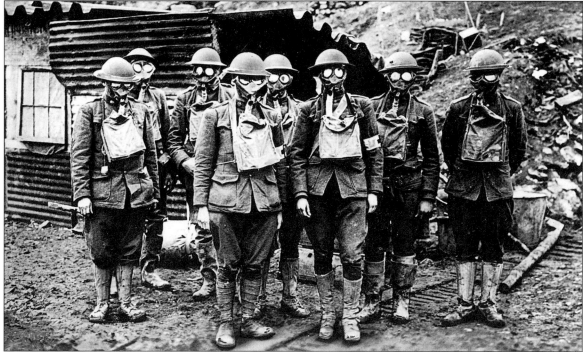

all Pershing's efforts to make the AEF stand alone as a fully self-defending force, it was humbled to find that its guns, tanks and airplanes were mostly "made in Europe," and that its assault tactics were deficient in many of the sophisticated features that the Europeans had so painfully evolved during four long years of battle. Nevertheless it discharged its duty with gallantry and honor, and won a major place in the peace conference held at Versailles during 1919.

ABOVE LEFT

*USS Hancock trooping to France in 1917. The assembly of Pershing's four million men would take a year to complete, which is a comparable rate to the six months needed to gather Schwarzkopf's half million in the more distant Persian Gulf, 1990-1. Deployment of 600,000 men to Vietnam between 1965 and 1967, however, was a disastrously slower operation.*

ABOVE RIGHT

*When they first went into action in France, American troops found themselves in the middle of a gas war that had been growing in intensity since 1915. Whereas the European allies had been able to accustom themselves gradually to this hazard, the inexperienced doughboys at first suffered exceptionally heavy gas casualties.*

*Practising a night trench attack in France with thermite (phosphorous) bombs, 15th August 1918. Phosphorous and napalm have continued to be important weapons in the US armory to this day.*

BELOW

*A US coastal artillery unit fires a long range railroad gun during the Argonne battle.*

*Raoul Lufberry, the air ace who started in the "French" American-manned Escadrille Lafayette before US entry into the war. He then went on to join the US 94th Aeropursuit Group (the Hat in the Ring squadron), and was finally credited with 17 kills. He also taught the art of advanced aerial combat to Pershing's chauffeur Eddie Rickenbacker... a pupil who would end the war with 26 kills.*

ABOVE

*Frank Luke, Jr., the American fighter ace credited with 21 kills.*

*A party of top war leaders on their way to the 1921 American Legion convention in Kansas City. Left to right: General Jacques of Belgium, General Diaz of Italy, Marshal Foch of France, General Pershing, and the British Admiral Beatty. Pershing was not only taller than the others, but he would also outlive them all.*

**ABOVE**

*General Pershing (second from left) reviews the A.E.F. in France with Secretary of War Newton D. Baker (in bowler hat). Pershing would eventually reach the unprecedented rank of "General of the Armies," higher even that George C. Marshall's "General of the Army" in WW2.*

**BELOW**

*President Wilson arrives with his wife at the Château de Versailles, to sign the peace treaty that he did so much to mold.*

France was not the only theater to which American troops were deployed during WW1. In the Cold War the Soviet Union would often recollect the Western allies' 1919 expeditions to prop up the counter-revolutionary White Armies in Russia. Pictured here is a machine gun company of the 31st US Infantry Regiment in Vladivostock, Siberia, the vital Soviet gateway to the Pacific.

A French-made 75 mm gun of the US 339th Infantry Regiment in North Russia, 1919.

The coming of peace is symbolized here by the return to the USA of the band of the 57th Artillery of New York, a unit that had made sweet music in all the big American battles in France.

# CHAPTER THREE

# "I WILL RETURN"

*—— MacArthur's campaigns from the Philippines to Guadalcanal and Back Again, 1941-5 ——*

Like many Europeans, Americans after 1918 hoped and believed that the World War had finally done away with the very idea of war itself. The United States set up the League of Nations, then effectively retired from power politics amid widespread questioning of whether the expeditionary force should ever have been sent to Europe at all. As late as 1937 – four years after Hitler had come to power in Germany and Japan had started her invasion of China – Congress was still passing yet another in a long series of neutrality acts. During much of this period the US regular army was frozen at around 130,000 men, or only marginally more than the 100,000 allowed to Germany under the terms of the Versailles treaty.

BELOW LEFT

*The annals of infamy are extended at Pearl Harbor, 7th December 1941. Here the 1921-vintage battleship USS* West Virginia *settles in the water after the Japanese attack, to be recommissioned in September 1944 and finally scrapped in 1961.*

BELOW

*3,000 US prisoners started on the infamous "Death March" through the jungle from Bataan in April 1942. Savagely treated and lacking food or water, few survived.*

Only gradually did public opinion come to accept eventual military intervention against fascism and imperialism in the wider world. It would be 1940 before rearmament was seriously undertaken, including the introduction of the nation's first peacetime draft in September. This gave a strength at the start of the war of about 1.5 million men – although that was still only about half of the Japanese total, and there were many deficiencies in training. At around the same time there was an escalation of US involvement in the Battle of the Atlantic and – most notably with the Lend-Lease bill of March 1941 – in support of the British and allied war effort. Both these measures gave a timely boost to US war industry and the first of 2,742 Liberty ships, for example, was ordered in January 1941. The USA also made strides forward in the field of military science, ranging from the 1939 commencement of the Manhattan Project to build an atomic bomb, all the way down to initiating research into radar, helicopters and guided missiles. The Army began to train and organize specialized armored and paratroop units, and to develop doctrines for their use.

America may thus have been taken by surprise when the Japanese attacked Pearl Harbor on 7th December 1941; but she was not entirely unprepared for war. She had already made more wide-ranging military preparations during peacetime than before any previous conflict. Nevertheless, the US tradition of last minute improvisation continued, since this new war soon turned out to be far more novel and demanding than any previous conflict. Diametrically opposite to their First World War record, for example, America's allies were now unable to furnish US soldiers with plentiful tanks and planes, but themselves presented an ever-lengthening list of requirements to Detroit and Seattle. Nor was it any longer enough for Uncle Sam to ship men overseas into secure base areas behind an existing fighting line. In this new war the fighting line itself often had to be established first, by a complex and dangerous beach assault operation. Once a line had been established, furthermore, the nature of modern mechanized combat turned out to be very different indeed from what had been learned in the past. The whole military machine therefore had to be built up from scratch according to new principles – usually while fierce fighting was still in progress. A vivid illustration of the need for reform came at Binalonan in the Philippines on 24th December 1941, when the 26th US Cavalry regiment actually launched a horsed cavalry charge against Japanese machine guns. Somewhat confusing for tactical analysts, however, was the fact that this attack succeeded in achieving its objectives!

The first US ground unit to be caught without

LEFT ABOVE

The USS San Francisco *brings down a Japanese aircraft off Guadalcanal, November 1942. The cruiser would later be badly damaged in this battle, but it survived the war.*

LEFT BELOW

*A temporary bridge on Guadalcanal fights a losing battle against rising flood water. A major problem throughout the Pacific campaign was the need to keep supply lines open despite poor roads and worse weather.*

BELOW

*Supplying the May 1943 assault on Attu Island, in the Aleutians, over the open beach. Quite apart from the fierce Japanese suicide attacks encountered in this battle, the mist and snow in the background belies the myth that every Pacific island was a sun-soaked paradise!*

adequate resources (and actually without "any visible means of support" at all) was the marine garrison of Wake Island, which was attacked on 7th December. The marines nevertheless managed to hold out heroically for sixteen days before being overwhelmed by superior numbers. Then it was the turn of the much larger Philippines, which were heavily bombed on 8th December and subjected to the first of a long series of amphibious landings on the 10th. Just as they had at Pearl, and at Hong Kong a day later, Japanese air attacks effectively destroyed the defending air force while it was still on the ground, thereby greatly easing the task of follow-on operations. By the end of December the US and Philippine ground forces, despite a quantitative if not qualitative superiority, had been forced to make a phased withdrawal through the island of Luzon to the defences of Manila. There they were besieged in the Bataan peninsula and the island fortress of Corregidor, largely cut off from both air and naval support by Japanese supremacy in the air.

The commander in the Philippines was General Douglas MacArthur, who had observed the 1905 Russo-Japanese War in Manchuria, led the 42nd "Rainbow" Division with distinction in France, 1917-18, and subsequently became the Army Chief of Staff. He was a flamboyant character, well aware of the value of self publicity; but also a shrewd and hard-headed strategist. In the agonising Philippines campaign of 1941-2 he exercised calm and strong control in a far from promising situation, drawing out the best from both his American and Filipino subordinates, and thereby allowing a firm defense to be set up at Bataan. Both overland attacks in front and amphibious attacks to the rear were then repelled, with the Japanese commander being forced to call up major reinforcements. MacArthur was persuaded to leave for a higher appointment only under protest, and by a direct order from the President. "I will return" was his defiant promise as he stepped aboard a PT boat for Mindanao on 17th March 1942.

Conditions among the besieged forces at Bataan were nonetheless appalling. Rations were short, enemy bombardment was continuous, and disease was running unchecked among the exhausted garrison. It was utterly remarkable that resistance could be maintained for no less than five months, with the enemy breakthrough coming only between 3rd and 9th April 1942 on the mainland, and the final surrender of Corregidor and all remaining forces in the Philippines being delayed until 6th May. MacArthur's heroic successor, General Jonathan M. Wainwright, then passed with his army into a state of captivity that all too few would survive – although the emaciated general would at least have the satisfaction of attending the eventual capitulation of Japan in 1945.

As for MacArthur himself, he made his way to Australia to take supreme command of the Southwest Pacific Area – now the principal focus of the US war effort in this theater. Admiral Chester W. Nimitz was simultaneously appointed supreme commander of the Pacific Ocean area – with the task of keeping open the sea lanes from Hawaii to Australia, and supporting MacArthur's efforts. The British took responsibility for India, Burma and Malaya, while the Kuomintang Generalissimo Chiang Kai Shek, aided by the American General Joseph W. ("Vinegar Joe") Stilwell, looked after China.

MacArthur's long term perspective was definitely offensive, since the origins of the war lay in US desires to reverse Japanese expansionism. He therefore wanted to leapfrog forward, from island to island, successively establishing a chain of air bases that could each secure the area, disrupt Japanese naval routes and isolate far-flung enemy garrisons. This "island hopping" technique was intended to penetrate the enemy's defensive barrier and eventually strike towards his homeland, but without necessarily having to

## THE PACIFIC THEATER

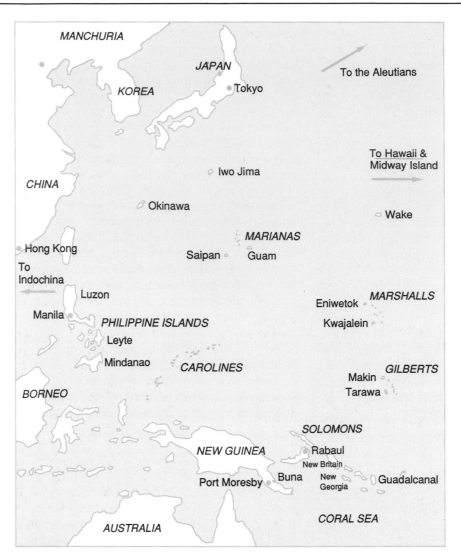

reduce every Japanese stronghold in the outer perimeter. Before their offensive could begin, however, the Americans' own line of communication first had to be secured against a new, three-pronged "island-hopping" attack mounted by the enemy. Elated by their winter successes, Hirohito's war leaders had started to revise their original plans. Instead of making a static defense on the positions already seized, they were now raising their sights and trying to extend their perimeter – lunging towards the Aleutians in the north, Midway Island in the center and Australia in the south.

Some of the Aleutian islands fell in June 1942; but the epochal battle of Midway was won by Nimitz' carriers at the start of the same month, guaranteeing the security of the central Pacific. However, a far more prolonged and bitter combat had already started around the shores of the Coral Sea – the gateway to Australia. From their new base at Rabaul on the eastern tip of the island of New Britain, seized in January, the Japanese were thrusting south to Port Moresby in Papua-New Guinea, and southeast towards Guadalcanal in the Solomons. If they succeeded in capturing these two points they would control the key allied supply line.

A direct Japanese amphibious lunge towards Port Moresby was headed off by the US Navy in the inconclusive Battle of the Coral Sea, in May. Then an overland thrust across New Guinea by several battalions was blocked by Australian troops on the steep Kokoda Trail in September. Finally, MacArthur launched a counter-attack in the swampy Buna area, on the coast at the eastern end of the Trail, where savage fighting continued over the winter, building up to Army Corps level. Buna fell in January 1943, allowing all the rest of the year to be taken up with an ever-growing series of allied air and amphibious assaults – sometimes including the novelty of paratroop drops – that secured many more footholds in New Guinea and on the western end of New Britain itself. The threat to Australia from this direction was therefore removed, although the

<hr>

RIGHT

*A water-cooled Browning .30 cal machine gun is dug in on Eniwetok Island, February 1944. An obsolescent M1903 Springfield rifle lies beside the gun.*

advance had been painfully slow due to all the logistic, training and acclimatization difficulties naturally associated with the improvisation of armies in distant and inhospitable theaters.

Nowhere, perhaps, was the theater quite as inhospitable as along the second Japanese axis of advance, from Rabaul through the Solomons to Guadalcanal. Here there were not only the same problems of jungle warfare, weather and disease as in Papua-New Guinea, but also the complicating danger of an enemy naval blockade that at times threatened to cut off all resupply. When General Alexander A. Vandergrift's marines first landed at Lunga Point on the north coast of Guadalcanal, on 7th August 1942, they found opposition deceptively weak. However, the Japanese soon responded by landing strong forces on either side of the beachead, covered by powerful naval attacks that initially chased off the Americans' supporting fleet and transports. For the next four months there was a cliff-hanger of a battle between Japanese ability to push home their assault, and US ability to consolidate their base and operate their airfield. It made a rare case of mutual, balanced but opposing amphibious landings on a distant shore – and by November each side had managed to place the equivalent of almost an Army Corps on the ground.

The Americans nevertheless eventually won the fight for Guadalcanal. Of decisive importance was the fierce naval campaign for control of the seas around the island. After months of fighting, the US Navy was eventually able to place an effective naval screen between friendly ground forces and the Japanese reinforcement convoys. This allowed Vandergrift to maintain both numerical and tactical superiority on land (with Army formations eventually joining the Marines); and he also exploited the power of a well-grouped defense against piecemeal assaults. Best of all, perhaps, the Americans successfully faced and overcame the horrors of full-blown jungle warfare, thereby creating a cadre of combat-hardened veterans that would fight at the spearhead of later battles. By January 1943 General Alexander McCarrell Patch was able to lead the breakout and pursuit from his XIV Corps perimeter, marking the first major American land victory of the war – and an indelible triumph in the annals of the Marine Corps. Overall there had been some 6,000 US casualties, to which must be added many more suffering from malaria – but Japanese losses were more than five times as high. During succeeding months US forces were able to leap-frog up the whole length of the Solomon chain, capturing New Georgia in July and half of Bougainville in November. They joined hands with the drive through New Guinea, and set the scene for more ambitious leaps forward in the following year.

Operations during 1944 fall into three general categories. Firstly the New Britain and New Guinea fronts had to be maintained and secured as bases for further action. Meanwhile Admiral Nimitz brought in fresh waves of US strike forces from Hawaii to seize key islands in the central Pacific. This theater was now given strategic priority, against the advice of the New Guinea-based MacArthur, since it offered a more direct line between Hawaii and the Philippines. Finally, towards the end of the year MacArthur and Nimitz joined hands for a major campaign to recapture the Philippines themselves. This would lead to ten months of successful – if attritional – ground fighting, that has somehow often been eclipsed in the popular imagination by the relatively smaller island assaults mounted to the north and east.

The New Guinea area was largely secure by September 1944, although some sizeable Japanese garrisons – including Rabaul itself – were bypassed to save losses, time and effort. Nevertheless the Australians had to be left behind to contain residual enemy forces in the area, and they understandably complained that they were still sustaining casualties even though the war had left them in a sideshow.

As for the central Pacific, planners realized it was much nearer to Hawaii than the New Guinea axis; yet if the Marianas could be captured they would provide air bases that were just as near to Tokyo as were the Northern Philippines. The result was a long succession of assault landing operations against defended islands, with the aim of establishing advanced airfields ever further towards the west. The northern flank in the Aleutians was cleared first, in July and August 1943. Then came the Gilberts, with Makin Atoll and "bloody Tarawa" in November 1943, followed by the Marshalls, from Kwajalein to Eniewetok, in the first two months of 1944. The Marianas themselves were secured in June and July, starting with the decisive naval battle of the Philippine Sea – "The Great Marianas Turkey Shoot" – which finally broke the back of Japanese naval aviation. This was quickly exploited by landings on Saipan, Tinian and Guam, and followed up in September and October by a new set of landings on the western end of the sprawling Caroline chain. As in the New Guinea campaign, many enemy garrisons were bypassed and, once deprived of air and naval strike capability, left to rot.

During these operations the technique of launching amphibious attacks over long distances was being invented almost from scratch, just as it was for much shorter distances in Europe at almost exactly the same time. Apart from the very different weather patterns, the main difference

LEFT

*The famous 2nd Marine Division comes out of the line on Saipan, late June 1944, for a short rest before returning in early July to repulse the final Japanese suicide charges. Infantry weapons include the .30 cal. self loading M1 carbine and M1 Garand rifle, both of which were vastly superior to Japanese rifles.*

between the two theaters was perhaps that the logistic assets needed to supply a Corps in Europe could scarcely maintain a division in the Pacific. The fleet train was thus developed to an enormous degree – on a scale that would cause the British Royal Navy to recoil in shock when it finally joined the island campaign in 1945. The British were used to mounting either small operations over long distances, or large operations over short distances – but here in the central Pacific during the last twelve months of the war the Americans had perfected a system for sustaining major operations over truly oceanic distances. We must remember that during WWII even the British and the Japanese navies could each produce only small handfuls of aircraft carriers or escort carriers – a score or so at best – but the Americans eventually managed to send more than 120 down *their* slipways.

When it came to amphibious assaults on defended islands, the first key principle was to isolate the enemy garrison from its supporting fleet or mobile reserves. This could be achieved through surprise, by feints to alternative targets or by the maximum exploitation of naval mobility; or it could be done simply by the destruction of enemy naval forces in an air-sea battle. All these techniques were used at one time or another in the Pacific campaign. Many lessons then had to be learned for the amphibious landings themselves; for example the need for loading troop transports "tactically," so that all the equipment needed in the first wave of the attack would be readily accessible, and only second echelon requirements would be stowed in the deepest holds. Drills also had to be worked out for the timing, alignment and rotation of the assault craft, to ensure that complete units could be landed all together and at the right places. At Tarawa many of them had been held at bay by the outer reef, so in later operations amphibious tractors were widely employed to overcome such obstacles. Continuity of resupply was another major headache, especially if the weather deteriorated or the supporting fleet was for some reason called away.

In tactical terms, doctrine called for the massive concentration of air and naval bombardment power against the beach defenses. If this could be supplemented by artillery fire from an offshore island, then so much the better. In scenes reminiscent of the Western Front during WWI, hundreds of tons of high explosive would be rained down on the Japanese bunkers over a period of days or even weeks. At Iwo Jima in February 1945 the naval gunfire preparation would last three days, and the preliminary air bombardment no less than 74 days. As on the Western Front, however, it was soon found that even the heaviest and longest preparatory assaults were unable completely to disarm a well dug in

ABOVE

*Marine Corps Sherman tanks being used as an improvised coastal battery. One of the many technological advantages enjoyed by the Americans over the Japanese was a considerable superiority in tank and anti-tank warfare.*

BELOW

*The 77th Division marches to the front at Yigo, northern Guam, in August 1944. Overall, the Marianas campaign would cost some 23,000 US casualties and almost 50,000 Japanese.*

defender. Deep bunker systems could withstand much of the onslaught, so the defending infantry would still be able to man its weapons against the incoming beach assault.

Interlocking fields of fire, arranged in depth over the whole surface of the disputed island, could slow the rate of advance to a snail's pace, and on some notorious occasions they produced an exceptionally heavy "butcher's bill." At Tarawa, for example, some 3,200 US casualties were sustained during the complete elimination of a Japanese garrison of about 4,500 strong. However, it must be said that in most assaults the ratio was far more favorable to the attacker than this. Learning by experience, the Americans developed a whole range of techniques for tackling these essentially static defenses in a careful and systematic way, notably by the use of tanks and liquid fire. In all the fighting through the Philippines, starting in late October 1944, there would be 60,000 US casualties to set against one third of a million enemy. Within these figures, furthermore, was concealed a "kill ratio" of no less than twenty four to one in favour of the Americans. There were few Japanese surrenders, and probably fewer still that were accepted. In this campaign, far more than in the war against Italy and Germany, the American soldier felt a psychic revulsion towards his fanatical and culturally alien enemy.

The re-occupation of the Philippines started when the two army corps of General Walter Krueger's Sixth Army landed in Leyte Gulf on 20th October 1944, quickly precipitating the climacteric naval battle of the same name. Total command of the air and sea was won by the battle, although this in itself did not give any great immediate advantages to the forces on the ground. Rain, mud, Japanese reinforcements – and even counter-attacks – delayed the final victory on Leyte island until the end of the year, with a "butcher's bill" of some 15,500 US casualties to set against 70,000 Japanese. Meanwhile, MacArthur pulled the Sixth Army out of the line for use in his next assault, against Luzon. This was unleashed on 9th January 1945, despite furious Kamikaze strikes, and followed very much the same line of attack as had been used by the Japanese to push the allies back on Manila in 1942. On this occasion, however, the Manila, Bataan and Corregidor defenses were successfully taken in the rear by seaborne and parachute assaults, and by the end of March the whole area had been cleared. Thus the "indirect approach" that MacArthur would later use at Inchon in 1950 was already a fully mature feature of his methods, and saved a great deal of time in these operations. Even so, the Japanese succeeded in maintaining a defense in the mountains to the north and east of Luzon, and in central Mindanao, right up to the end of the war.

ABOVE

*The first US flag raised in the assault on on the Leyte beaches in the Philippines, 20th October 1944.*

BELOW

*San Francisco Coastguardsman Frank Cuenca writes a first hand report on the fighting for the Leyte beaches. Eyewitness accounts of incoming fire are more normally written after the event, rather than during it.*

Two major island assault operations remained to be mounted as the ring of American air bases closed in on Japan. Although heavy B-29 bombers could already hit Tokyo from the Marianas, they could not be escorted to the target, supported by medium bombers or given emergency rescue at any point midway onwards in their flight. Nor could the final landings on the Japanese mainland – Operations "Olympic" and "Coronet," planned for November 1945 and March 1946 respectively – be contemplated without bases closer to the objective than were currently available. It was for all these reasons, therefore, that the assault on Iwo Jima was set for 19th February 1945, and that on Okinawa for 1st April.

Iwo Jima was a painfully obvious target, since it was the only practicable site for an airfield within more than 1,200 miles of the southern and eastern coasts of Japan. It was scarcely more than four miles long, but it was defended by some 21,000 Japanese troops who had spent a very long time turning the whole place into a veritable rabbit warren of deep fortifications and gun positions. Only three reinforced marine divisions made the assault (the 3rd, 4th and 5th), which gave them less than the three to one force ratio normally considered a minimum safe level for an attacker. It took them over a month to eliminate the opposition, making an average rate of advance of about one mile per week. Almost all the Japanese were killed; but the Americans suffered some 24,000 casualties – half their strength – of which nearly 7,000 were killed in action. Iwo Jima was certainly a valuable prize – but it was a mighty expensive one.

Next came Okinawa, where General Simon B. Buckner Jr. landed some six divisions of his Tenth Army on 1st April. Starting at a point a third of the way up the 50-mile long island, the initial assault was unexpectedly successful. The airfields of Yontan and Kadena were quickly secured, and 6th Marine Division was able to occupy the whole northern part of the island without encountering consolidated resistance. Further south, however, the story was different. The Japanese had established strong defenses across the island – the Machinato Line – which they intended to hold while a massed Kamikaze attack removed the supporting fleet from Buckner's rear. In the event the Kamikazes did sink 20 ships and damaged 157 more, but they ultimately failed to dislodge the American naval presence around the islands. When the mighty battleship *Yamato* tried to intervene, it was sunk by carrier aircraft. The US ground forces were thus left free to move forward to the assault.

The battle for southern Okinawa was long and bloody. By the end of April the fighting had penetrated less than two miles beyond the Machinato Line, and the Tenth Army had to halt

*The battle-hardened 77th Division comes ashore from "Landing Craft Infantry" (LCIs) for yet another gruelling island battle – this time on Leyte, late 1944. On this occasion the division was used as MacArthur's amphibious spearhead for wide-flanking exploitation after other formations had engaged the enemy in frontal battle.*

to regroup. This pause encouraged the enemy to launch a costly counter-attack that consumed his slender reserves; but when the US advance was resumed, it made little better progress than before. During May Buckner encountered a new cluster of formidable fortifications, the Shuri line, and in terrible weather conditions was able to win only four more miles of real estate. However, the 96th Division eventually managed to capture Conical Hill, which was the key to the eastern flank of the position, so by the start of June there seemed to be a new glimmer of hope. The town of Naha fell, and the enemy retreated to his final redoubt on the southern tip of the island. Here he was run to earth and destroyed before the end of the month, making for a total loss in the battle of more than 118,000 Japanese troops, all but 7,000 of whom were killed in action. Against this must be set

some 49,000 US casualties, including 12,500 killed in action. Among the latter was the ill-starred Buckner himself. The son of the Confederate general who had surrendered Fort Donelson in 1862, he was killed on the 18th June, only a few days before his forces at last overcame what was perhaps the most heavily fortified position of the whole Pacific war.

With the capture of Iwo Jima and Okinawa, the strategic bombing of Japan could move into top gear. From March 1945 onwards there was a remorseless round of accurate incendiary attacks that gutted many of the cities and presaged the destruction to be wrought by the two atomic bombs – on 6th August against Hiroshima, and on 9th August against Nagasaki. Thus was the war brought to an end before it was necessary to mount Operations "Olympic" and "Coronet."

The rights and wrongs of strategic bombing, not to mention nuclear first use, have become ever more questionable with the passage of time. Both these cruel processes were nevertheless hailed with great enthusiasm in 1945 by the men who had fought their way through so many dense enemy bunker systems. These were men who knew the full horrors of close-quarter combat in this unforgiving theater, and they were heartily glad to be relieved of its burden, by whatever means.

ABOVE

General Douglas MacArthur explains things during the Philippines invasion to Lieutenant General Walter Krueger, commanding 6th Army, and Vice Admiral Thomas C. Kincaid, commanding 7th Fleet.

TOP

Bloody carnage on the beach at Iwo Jima following the 5th Marine Amphibious Corps' assault on 19th February 1945. The battle for the island would last more than a month and at 24,000 US casualties it would actually cost more than the 21,000 Japanese defenders.

ABOVE

Men of the 5th Marine Division display Japanese flags captured in hard fighting during the initial assault on Iwo Jima. This was the division that would later – memorably and sculpturally – capture Mount Suribachi and raise the American flag on the rim of the crater.

BELOW

BELOW

*A Marine 105 mm howitzer shelling Japanese positions on Iwo Jima.*

RIGHT

*Smoke rising from preparatory bombing of Toguchi, Okinawa, by carrier-based US Navy aircraft, 1st April 1945. The battle started well but soon bogged down into some of the most ferocious trench warfare of the entire campaign. It would cost a total of some 49,000 American casualties.*

FAR RIGHT

*The terminal Nagasaki bomb of 9th August 1945. The Pacific war turned out to be the world's only atomic war for two main reasons. On one hand the USA had just invented the bomb and was anxious to show it to the world; on the other hand the experience of Iwo Jima and Okinawa had shown that American infantry casualties could be prohibitive in the face of deeply dug-in defenders. In a way reminiscent of Grant's frustrated recourse to scorched earth in 1864, therefore, the tactical victories of the island-hopping campaign were misinterpreted in Washington as costly defeats that could be redeemed only by the wholesale devastation of enemy cities.*

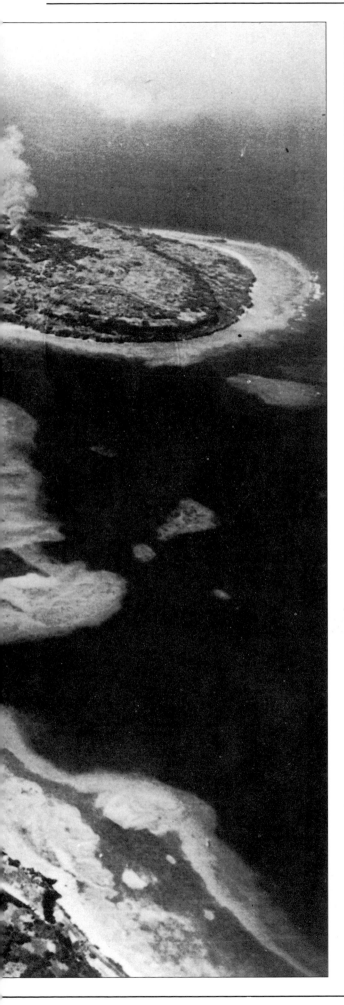

# CHAPTER FOUR

# TESTING "THE SOFT UNDERBELLY" AT KASSERINE AND CASSINO

*The Mediterranean Theater, 1942-5*

I f America was brought into the war by Japanese aggression at Pearl Harbor, it was against Germany that President Franklin D. Roosevelt wanted to direct the major part of her military power. Germany was seen as potentially a far more dangerous rival to the USA, since she commanded enormously greater industrial and technological resources than did Japan. If the USSR had collapsed under the weight of Hitler's 1942 offensive – as she might well have done – there would have been little that Britain on her own could have done to prevent the establishment of a Nazi super-state covering most of continental Europe.

ABOVE

*The army that General Eisenhower shipped directly across the Atlantic to the Torch landings in North Africa, November 1942, had only a theoretical understanding of modern warfare. Here a naval petty officer converts to the mentality required of an Army officer, at West Point.*

*Landing craft ferrying troops onto the North African beaches from their mother ship, a "Landing Ship Tank" (LST). They are directed by semaphore from the shore in what was the first in a long series of amphibious landings in the Mediterranean and European theaters.*

The "Germany First" policy was hotly contested by many senior figures, not least MacArthur himself, and in practice a much greater proportion of US resources were bled away to the Pacific war than Roosevelt would have wished. Nevertheless, the general principle remained intact, and an early start was made on the planning of a large scale invasion of Europe, to relieve pressure on Russia and topple the Nazi regime as rapidly as possible. The idea was to launch Operation "Sledgehammer," a frontal attack on France through the Cherbourg peninsula. The British, however, insisted that such an undertaking would be foolhardy in the extreme, at least in the conditions of 1942. Not only would the assault forces be lacking in experience, cohesion and specialist equipment; but they would be making a head-on assault against the most efficient army in the world at the very height of its strength. Instead of France itself, therefore, the British wanted the 1942 operation to be directed against the much more modest target of French North Africa.

At first this suggestion was met with incredulity, since the enemy in such an operation would not be Germans at all, but Frenchmen. Admittedly the British had already fought a series of skirmishes against this foe, not least of which was the sinking of the Mers el Kebir fleet in 1940. The Americans, however, hoped that that an accommodation could still be made, and suspected their British allies of harboring deep imperialist designs in the whole Mediterranean region. It certainly seemed ludicrous that the first major US offensive in response to a Japanese attack on Hawaii should be directed against the French in Africa! On careful analysis, however, "Sledgehammer" did indeed seem to be impractical, so US planners eventually fell in with the plan to occupy Morocco, Algeria and Tunisia. At first this was codenamed Operation "Super-Gymnast" (following an earlier, all-British plan for "Gymnast"); but by the time of its execution on 8th November it had become known as Operation "Torch."

"Torch" was commanded by General Dwight D. Eisenhower, a former subordinate of both

ABOVE RIGHT

*A light anti-aircraft gun comes ashore at Arzeu near Oran, Algeria, in Operation Torch.*

RIGHT

*GIs raring to get ashore near Oran, November 1942, in what the official caption breezily called the "opening of the second front." For most people, however, the true "second front" would not begin until the D-Day landings in June 1944.*

MacArthur and Marshall, with General Mark W. Clark as second in command and General Patton in charge of the beach landings around Casablanca. Exceptionally close liaison arrangements were also in place with the British. Thus the staff team that would run the war in the West right through until final victory in 1945 was already assembled in embryo; and in the event the experience it gained in North Africa would stand it in very good stead throughout the still tougher battles that were to come. Exactly as in the Far East, in fact, it was experience of real combat that was to be the allies' most valuable acquisition during 1942-3.

"Torch" turned out to be a classic case of "over-insurance," since a major intervention by Spanish and German troops from Spanish Morocco was feared right up to the last minute. The US forces landing around Casablanca in French Morocco and Oran in Western Algeria were therefore initially given a defensive role, while the Anglo-American task force that went for Algiers city was held back from an early seizure of the vital ports in Tunisia, further to the east. This caution was not in fact necessary, since no Spanish intervention actually took place, and the French agreed to a ceasefire after just two days' fighting. Instead, the failure to seize Tunisia turned out to have been a serious mistake, because the Germans were able to send in reinforcements to hold a line in the steep mountain area covering the ports of Tunis and Bizerte. The allies had to fight a long and hard campaign through the winter before they could finally occupy the key terrain.

Despite achieving strategic surprise, the "Torch" landings still had to contend with dangerously high seas and active French defenses. *Coup de main* forces at both Oran and Algiers suffered heavy casualties when they tried to seize the port facilities under the noses of the defense, while Patton's beach landing at Port Lyautey, seventy miles north of Casablanca, was also stalled for two days by the ferocity of the French riposte. It was only when tanks could be landed, and the other assaults around Casablanca had undermined resistance, that progress inland could be made. Of the 1,404 US casualties suffered in "Torch" as a whole, over half were on the Morocco front.

After "Torch" came the race for Tunis, which was won by the Germans. The allied advance was halted by a counter-attack at the end of November, and a "trenchlock" soon set in, exposed to bitterly cold and wet winter conditions. In the bleak Tunisian hills every attack tended to be channelled into narrow valleys overlooked by steep slopes that the Germans had fortified and tank-proofed. Added to this was a strong *Luftwaffe* challenge to allied command of the air, and the arrival of the first in a powerful new generation of heavy tanks

ABOVE

*Senior American and French officers inspecting damage at the US residence in Casablanca, Morocco, after the hard-fought Torch landings in this sector.*

– the dreaded Pzkw VI Tiger. Whereas at El Alamein in October the British General Bernard Montgomery's Eighth Army's M4 Shermans had represented an important technical advance over any German tank then in the field, already by the time of the Tunisian campaign the Sherman was starting to look distinctly obsolete. This was to be a major handicap to the Western allies for most of the remainder of the war, since the Sherman would be effectively superseded by more advanced designs – notably the M26 Pershing – only in the very last months of hostilities.

By February 1943, the allied line in Tunisia, under the overall direction of British General Kenneth A. N. Anderson's First Army, looked over-extended and shaky. Not only did its nine divisions have a frontage almost 250 miles long, but it was composed of a somewhat disparate array of French colonial, British and American forces, practically none of whom had previously seen action, let alone collaborated in such an alliance. The initiative seemed to have passed to the Germans, whose repeated local spoiling attacks kept sending shudders along the allied line. The biggest and most impressive of these began on 14th February, when a dual thrust was mounted from east and south simultaneously towards the American communications center at Kasserine.

LEFT

*German Pzkw Mk III tanks destroyed in the US counter-attack at Kasserine, late February 1943. The initial German onslaught had come as a jarring initiation into the realities of modern armored warfare, but in succeeding weeks Eisenhower's legions were gradually able to find their feet and participate in an overwhelming victory in Tunis.*

BELOW

*General Patton attends maneuvers of a unit of M3 Stuart light tanks, North Africa May 1943. Although vastly better than the French Renault light tanks with which he had served in WWI, by 1943 the Stuart had been seriously outclassed by German anti-tank defenses.*

The main assault came frontally from the east, spearheaded by two panzer divisions under General Juergen von Arnim. These initially sliced through the US 1st Armored Division and pressed forward some 40 miles in four days, amid scenes of panic and confusion on the American side. As its first major exposure to the "big league" of modern warfare, this experience may well be compared to the AEF's discomfiture at Belleau Wood in 1918. As on the earlier occasion, however, American resilience and determination won through in the end and, with the help of British reinforcements, an effective defense was consolidated in each of the four valleys down which the enemy was trying to push. On the German side, by contrast, the initial impetus was gradually dissipated by a combination of over-extension, over-dispersion, and command disunity. Although von Arnim had made all the running at the start of the operation, he was soon upstaged by General Erwin Rommel, "the desert fox," whose Afrika Korps had advanced from the south to seize Kasserine itself. Rommel thereafter made the deepest penetrations towards the west, but in the process he disrupted the German chain of command by claiming overall seniority in the theater. This would be granted only two weeks later, when the fruits of the operation had already been thrown away. His withdrawal from the Kasserine area began on 22nd February, only a week after the offensive had begun.

Perhaps the biggest difference between the US military experience in the Pacific theater and that in the West was the readiness of the enemy to launch effective counter-attacks. On their Pacific atolls the Japanese usually relied almost entirely upon static fortifications, and would make "Banzai charges" only as desperate, last ditch measures. When they did so, furthermore, they would use only infantry, light artillery and, at best, light tanks. These could usually be brushed aside

quickly by infantry alone, and would therefore often serve to boost the morale of the defense as much as they exhausted that of the attackers. In the western theater, by contrast, the Germans believed in making systematic counter-attacks with all arms and at all times. Their armament was better and heavier than the Japanese at every level, and their concept of operations was notably dynamic rather than static. Thus, as soon as an American attack had overrun some front line bunkers, German doctrine would require an immediate counter-attack by infantry supported by heavy tanks, heavy mortars and heavy artillery – not to mention air power if it was available. This made the Germans a much trickier opponent to deal with at the tactical level than the Japanese, even though they were often more logistically accessible than the latter's widely-scattered Pacific garrisons.

By 20th March 1943 the initiative in Tunisia nevertheless swung back to the allies, as Montgomery began his operation to break through the Mareth Line. Meanwhile, Patton had taken command of US II Corps, tasked with pinning down the 10th Panzer Division. At first his 1st Armored Division conducted an effective defense – in gratifying contrast to its performance in the February battle – then he moved into the counter-attack with the 1st, 9th and 34th Infantry Divisions. These joined hands with Montgomery's pursuit forces on 7th April; but a skilled German rearguard action – now once again under von Arnim – ensured that no major enemy formation could be entrapped in southern Tunisia.

Instead, the entire German-Italian Army Group Africa, with some sixteen divisions and almost a third of a million men, became entrapped in a small pocket around the city of Tunis itself. Pushed back on all sides by a general allied offensive, the Axis line buckled and cracked. The British at the center and right of the line made disappointingly slow progress; but both the French on the right center and the Americans on the left made good headway. Now under the command of General Omar N. Bradley, US II Corps captured the commanding Hill 609 and then pressed forward to seize the communications node at Mateur on 3rd April. Despite some bitter reverses, Bradley went on to take the port of Bizerte by 7th April, thereby making an important contribution to the overall disintegration of the enemy defenses. The final surrender of Tunisia came on 13th April, marking a loss to the German war effort that was almost as damaging as that of Stalingrad three months earlier, albeit far less noticed. In neither case had Hitler authorised an evacuation until it was too late, with the result that he needlessly squandered irreplaceable armies.

With the whole of North Africa clear of the enemy, the question was where the allies should strike next. The Americans had argued once again for northern France; but since so many forces were already committed to the Mediterranean they had agreed to settle for the south of that country, instead. The British, however, were still unready to tackle "the big one" and had pressed for the Balkans. In January 1943, therefore, the Casablanca conference had chosen Sicily and Italy as the best possible compromise between the two. The first operation, codenamed "Husky," would be a landing in southeastern Sicily by approximately eleven divisions divided between Montgomery's British Eighth Army, on the right, and Patton's American Seventh Army on the left. The attack would be prepared by a massive air interdiction and counter-air bombardment designed to wreck Axis runways and overland communications.

Under cover of bad weather and an elaborate deception plan, the assault forces secured their beachheads as planned in the early morning of 10th July 1943, encountering very little opposition. They were greatly helped by a whole new generation of amphibious assault equipment, ranging from the classic Landing Ship Tank (or LST) down to the humble, but no less classic, DUKW. They were also supported by the first allied paratroop operation on a genuinely large scale, although in this case the results were mixed. In their first drop the airborne soldiers were widely scattered by the high winds, but they did still reach most of their objectives and materially contributed to the enemy's sense of disorientation.

In subsequent drops, however, they suffered from an understandable lack of experience in this novel style of warfare, and sometimes came under "friendly" anti-aircraft fire – with the tragic loss of hundreds of men. As with any new weapon, the paras found there must be a long and painful learning process before full and correct techniques and tactics could be developed.

On 11th July the Germans mounted a dangerous counter-attack supported by powerful air strikes; but they were eventually beaten off by heavy fire, especially from the fleet. The allies were thus allowed to complete their unloading, as the enemy gradually retreated to a redoubt in the northeastern corner of the island, around Catania and the Mount Etna massif. Patton's men were thus left free to force march to Palermo, which they entered in triumph on 22nd July. This could not, however, accelerate progress through the close and difficult terrain in the front line. The Germans executed an exemplary fighting

*Operation Husky, the July 1943 landing in Sicily. Although ultimately successful, this over-extended invasion could call on too few landing craft, and served to remind the allied forces that they still had much to learn about warfare in the "big league." It nevertheless proved that an amphibious landing could be made to work even without access to a major port – a lesson that would make the invasion of Normandy possible eleven months later.*

withdrawal, learning to trade space for time in very much the same way as they were doing in Russia during this same summer of 1943. Given a plentiful supply of mines, anti-tank guns and Spandau teams, they were able to put up a daunting resistance in every field and every village. Not even a series of allied amphibious landings in their rear could prevent a smooth Axis evacuation of more than 100,000 men across the straits of Messina between 3rd and 17th August. They left behind some 141,000 killed, wounded and prisoners, however, for a total cost of some 23,000 casualties to the allies – surely a very profitable rate of exchange for the attacking army. Still better, the campaign in Sicily led to the final collapse of Mussolini and his replacement by the peace-minded Marshal Pietro Badoglio.

Eisenhower hastened to capitalize on the change in the Italian regime, by launching multiple assault landings on the Italian mainland early in September. In particular, four US and British divisions went ashore at Salerno on the 9th in Operation "Avalanche," despite stubborn resistance by the 16th Panzer Division. The green US 36th Division was particularly badly handled, although it did manage to reach its initial objectives. In successive days the German commander, Field Marshal Albert Kesselring, rushed reinforcements into the ring of hills surrounding the narrow beaches. The allies were totally overlooked and subjected to continuous artillery and mortar fire. A series of heavy German counter-attacks pushed them back from the much-disputed tobacco factory and hill 424, and on 13th September even threatened to throw the whole allied force back into the sea. There were over 1,000 US casualties, and three times as many British. The only reinforcements that could be sent in time were two battalions of the 82nd Airborne Division that were parachuted into the beachhead.

Fortunately the line was consolidated by 15th September and Kesselring, lacking the strength to do more, began to pull away. This signalled the start of a great allied trudge up the whole length of Italy, from Naples to Venice and Milan, that would last for most of the next two wearisome years. Moving against the grain of the country, from one heavily defended ridgeline to the next, the advance would be hampered by poor roads, bad weather, liberally-scattered enemy mines, and the depressing sense that this theater was just a sideshow, holding very secondary priority to the Normandy landings that were being prepared for the summer of 1944.

From the Salerno beachhead it took two months to advance sixty miles to Kesselring's "Winter Line," still only half way to Rome. Hard fighting and two more months were needed to penetrate this and push on to the "Gustav Line" ten miles

behind. Hence it would be 15th January 1944 before the allies finally came up against the Rapido river and the dominating bastion of Monte Cassino, topped by the founding monastery of the Benedictine order, which completely barred the way to all further advance.

The four epic battles of Monte Cassino were polyglot affairs in which a dozen different nationalities participated, including Algerians, Moroccans, South Africans and Indians, Canadians, New Zealanders, French and Poles.

*Throughout the Mediterranean campaign the US forces operated alongside the British "Desert Rats," the Royal Air Force and the Royal Navy. Here the British come ashore on Sicily as an integral part of Operation Husky.*

*Patton takes yet another puff of his cigar after successfully defending Gela, on the southern coast of Sicily, against a powerful German counter-attack. This difficult action opened the road north to Palermo.*

There were even Italians, fighting against their former allies who now seemed hell-bent on turning the whole of Italy into a battlefield. Amid all these diverse contingents the Americans played only a relatively minor part, with just the 36th Division leading the initial attack across the Rapido on 20th January. Poor organization and terrible weather conspired to make this a bloody failure with 1,700 casualties – yet another reverse for an outfit that had already been mauled at Salerno. Then in early February the 34th US Division

**ABOVE: THE MEDITERRANEAN THEATER**

*A warm welcome for "Old Glory" as US forces liberate Aragona, Sicily.*

**RIGHT: MONTE CASSINO AND THE ANZIO BRIDGEHEAD**

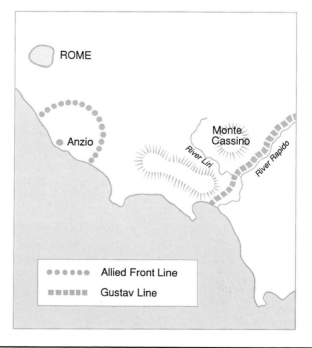

Allied Front Line
Gustav Line

attempted to capture the area of Cassino itself, but with no better result and 2,400 more casualties. This was a stronghold that would repel repeated allied assaults for many months to come.

A much greater US contribution came in Operation "Shingle," the amphibious assault on the Germans' rear at Anzio, in the early hours of 22nd January. General John P. Lucas' VI Corps landed successfully and seemed to pose a direct threat both to Rome and to Kesselring's line of communication to the Cassino front. Whether for good reasons or bad – and the point has been much debated – he did not leap forward to exploit his position quickly, but first spent a week securing his beachhead and landing supplies. When he was finally ready to break out, he found himself encircled by enemy divisions that had been hastily, but no less effectively, assembled. A long battle of attrition set in, amid scenes reminiscent of the Western Front of 1914-18. Lucas was soon replaced by General Lucian K. Truscott Jr., his former subordinate.

Whatever else it did or did not achieve, the Anzio operation at least drew off German resources not only from the Cassino front – thereby making the eventual breakout easier – but also from other theaters. It raised the value of the Italian war as a strategic diversion, yet did not prevent many of the precious landing craft being

ABOVE

*An American self-propelled howitzer moving forward through Palma, Sicily, July 1943.*

LEFT

*The massed aerial bombing of the unique medieval monastery of Monte Cassino, 25th February 1944. This dominating hilltop position had already held up the allied advance for over a month, and despite the bombing would continue to do so for a further four months – a clear reminder that protracted trench warfare had by no means been made obsolete by the end of WWI.*

returned to England in time for the D-Day invasion. When the allies' offensive impetus was finally regained in May, furthermore, the Anzio beachhead had been crammed with troops who were raring to lead the advance. As the Cassino position was outflanked to the south, Clark's Fifth Army was able to join hands with them as they drove forward to Rome. Despite an overall US loss of 20,000 casualties in this month-long operation, they successfully liberated the eternal city on 4th June, just two days before the Normandy landings.

After Cassino, Anzio and Rome the German forces in Italy were far from destroyed, and could find many more ridgelines to defend, stretching all the way back to the Alps. The allies had nevertheless reached Florence by the start of August and had penetrated the Gothic line by October – but there they halted just a few miles short of Bologna and the Po valley, exhausted by uphill fighting and a steady drain of losses. The Americans alone suffered some 16,000 casualties in six weeks. Seven of the best allied divisions had also been stripped away to invade the south of France in Operation "Anvil," and the winter rains were turning the roads into quagmires. It would not be until April 1945 that the advance could be resumed. The British Eighth Army led off on 2nd April on the eastern side of the country, to be followed on the 14th by the US Fifth Army, now commanded by Truscott. His 10th Mountain Division distinguished itself by its rapid infiltrations on foot, opening a path into the plains through which the armor could burst out to exploit the situation. From 20th April mobility was dramatically restored to the front as the remnants of the German defenses were shattered and the allies pursued remorselessly to north and west. Within ten days they were at the foot of the Alps, and the liberation of Italy was complete.

ABOVE LEFT

*In order to undo the deadlock at Monte Cassino an amphibious landing at Anzio, in the enemy's rear, was mounted on 22nd January 1944. Churchill said he had wanted to throw a wildcat ashore, to capture Rome, but found instead that he had only a "beached whale."*

LEFT

*The Anzio beachhead quickly sank into a trench deadlock every bit as deadly and indecisive as the fighting at Cassino. At the end of April the DUKWs ferrying in supplies were still within range of damaging enemy artillery fire.*

*LSTs supplying the troops at Anzio through the shattered heart of the port, March 1944.*

*American soldiers cautiously removing demolition charges from buildings near the Anzio docks, making a pile of explosive at their feet.*

*Ultimate victory in the Italian campaign included the tasteless display of the murdered Mussolini and his mistress hanging by their heels in central Milan. Adolf Hitler would take great care to avoid a similar fate.*

# CHAPTER FIVE

# VICTORY IN EUROPE

*Eisenhower's campaigns from Normandy to Bavaria, 1944-5*

W hile the Anglo-American forces in Italy were still floundering towards the fortified hillsides of the Gustav Line, the veteran leaders of the Mediterranean war – Eisenhower, Bradley, Patton and Montgomery – slipped quietly away to prepare for Operation "Overlord" – the Normandy invasion. This was to be the greatest amphibious assault of all time, involving over 4,000 vessels, 14,000 aircraft – including 2,000 heavy bombers – and a total of almost three million men, of whom around 150,000 would land on D-Day itself, including three airborne divisions.

As the Normandy battle continues in July 1944, the Free French leader Charles de Gaulle meets veteran US commander John J. Pershing in the Walter Reed Military Hospital.

(From left to right) Supreme Allied Commander General Dwight D. Eisenhower, British Prime Minister Winston S. Churchill, and Lieutenant General Omar N. Bradley, get to know each other better in 1944 by trying out the US M1 carbine together.

The operation was meticulously planned, with reconnaissance and intelligence collection in unprecedented depth; a major air interdiction campaign to destroy enemy communications all around the battlefield; and intensive training exercises in southern England, although, tragically, in one such exercise some 749 US soldiers died when their landing craft were torpedoed by enemy E-boats. Apart from all this, a major campaign was mounted to deceive and baffle the enemy as to the strategic plan. Patton's "Third Army" was set up as just a skeleton headquarters at Dover, issuing radio emissions and other fake signatures to suggest that the main invasion would be across the *Pas de Calais*, and hence that the Normandy attack was only a preliminary diversion. So successful was this piece of disinformation that Hitler continued to retain very strong reserves in the Calais area throughout the two months of the decisive battle further south – a very important contributory factor in allied success. In the event, of course, Patton would be inserted secretly into the Normandy beachhead after the initial landings, and would lead the real Third Army in the spearhead of the final breakout in late July.

Even the best laid plans can come unstuck, however, and "Overlord" was not without its share of setbacks. The first of these was the uncertain state of the weather for 5th June, which led to a day's cancellation of the attack. When the same problem was raised again for 6th June, however, Eisenhower took the resolute decision to go ahead anyway, even in marginal weather. This added materially to the degree of tactical surprise, but it meant that the landing took place in choppy seas and with a high incidence of sea sickness, and unfortunate problems of station-keeping. Despite these difficulties the gamble did pay off, and a window of relatively clear weather was found for the initial landings to become properly established. Two weeks later, however, a severe storm disrupted the unloading program for more than four days, and broke up the two prefabricated "Mulberry" harbors that had been established off the beaches. This led to a grave crisis in the logistic plan that was intensified by the failure to capture French ports within the timescales required. The Germans had placed exceptionally strong garrisons in each of the ports along the Channel coast, and each garrison proved to be far more efficient at blocking the waterways and demolishing the dockyard plant than the allies had expected. Eisenhower would never have sufficient port facilities for his logistic requirements until at least the opening of Antwerp at the end of November, and this consideration would radically affect the shape of all his operations.

Nor did the upsets to "Overlord" stop with

It was helped in this by two divisional paratroop drops designed to secure the low-lying marshland behind the beach. Despite considerable scattering due to cloud and anti-aircraft fire, the paratroops secured most of their objectives apart from two bridges around the town of Carentan. The 101st Airborne Division seized key ground for 4th Division's advance, and also the vital lock near Carentan that the Germans might have used to flood the whole area. The 82nd Airborne Division took St. Mère Eglise amid heavy fighting, but left two regiments scattered and besieged on the far side of the river Merderet. It would be several days before they could be rescued. Overall US casualties on D-Day in this area were about 2,700, almost all among the airborne forces.

After D-Day, Bradley's US First Army had two main objectives. It had to seize the key port of Cherbourg to its right rear, and it had to press forward to take territory towards the south. Meanwhile, Montgomery's British Second Army, on the left, would advance in step with the Americans through Caen towards the south and east.

The capture of Cherbourg was entrusted to VII Corps, commanded by General J. Lawton Collins, a veteran of Guadalcanal. Systematically advancing in narrow columns through close country, he reached the city on 20th June and took it by the 27th, albeit with the loss of some 22,000 casualties in the entire operation since D-Day. However, because of German demolitions the port could not be operated until 7th August, over a month later than had been hoped.

When it came to the main frontal advance to the south, however, the picture was gloomier still. Not only were resources being diverted into the Cherbourg operation, but the terrain consisted of *bocage;* a patchwork of small fields criss-crossed with leafy hedgerows set on top of thick earth banks. This formed a natural version of the honeycombed earthworks that had been seen on many battlefields in the Civil War, and then on the Western Front. Progress through defended *bocage* was almost impossible for tanks, as they could be ambushed from the foliage by *panzerfausts,* and it was little easier for the infantry. German snipers and Spandau teams, dug deep into the solid earth banks, could spring to life from unexpected directions at any time. Artillery strikes also lost a great deal of their effect due to the restricted vision of observers and the strength of the defender's fortifications.

When Bradley's men encountered the *Bocage* their initial impetus could carry them only a short distance into it. By 13th June the enemy had consolidated a defensive line between ten and twenty miles inland from the beaches – including the crescent of high ground north of St. Lô – and there he held fast. By 24th July, six weeks later, he

ABOVE LEFT

*British Field Marshal Bernard Montgomery, who held overall tactical command of the initial allied landings in Normandy, appreciates a pet goldfish sent by approving WWI veterans in Missouri, November 1944.*

ABOVE

*(From left to right) Eisenhower watches D-Day rehearsals alongside the British Air Marshal Tedder and Field Marshal Montgomery.*

LEFT

*Omar N. Bradley, an important – albeit somewhat eclipsed – player in the allied victory in Europe. He commanded the successful US 1st Army with distinction, then was promoted to command 12th Army Group – a post equal in rank to Montgomery, who commanded 21st Army Group.*

these metereological and logistic difficulties. On D-Day itself there was a generally poor rate of advance from the beaches, and by D plus 60 the front line had lagged almost 150 miles behind the plan. The whole German defensive scheme, and the terrain in which it was emplaced, simply turned out to be far harder to crack than the planners had ever imagined. The initial US landing on Omaha beach was a classic case in point, since the defenders were twice as strong as had been anticipated, and managed to survive the preliminary air bombardment almost unscathed due to the bad visibility. When the US 1st and then 29th Infantry Divisions came into the assault up the steep beach, they encountered great difficulties with obstacles, the dispersion of the assault battalions and the fact that all too many of their tanks and DUKWs had sunk while attempting to come ashore. Thousands of troops were pinned to the ground by raking machine gun fire from the overlooking cliffs, and some 2,000 became casualties. It was only after many hours, and through stupendous feats of personal heroism, that the forward movement could be reanimated at all. Even then, it would have come to naught if the Germans had elected to make a major counter-attack at this point – but in the event they did not do so, simply because they believed they had already won game, set and match.

On Utah beach further to the west there was a much happier picture, as 4th Division got ashore and overcame enemy resistance relatively easily.

had been pushed back only a few miles, with St. Lô itself falling only on 18th July. Casualties reached a combined allied total for First and Second armies of some 122,000 since D-Day, and it began to look as though Operation "Cobra" – the planned breakout west of St. Lô – would never come about.

Come about it did, however, when Collins' VII Corps made an initially limited advance towards Coutances on 25th July. There were serious problems with the carpet of bombs laid down by the air force ahead of the attack, since it sometimes crept back and hit friendly troops as well as German defenders. There were 558 casualties, including one general killed, to this cause. Nevertheless the bombardment did pulverize the enemy, and his lack of reserves in depth at this point was clearly exposed. After two days' fighting his front had collapsed and the Americans were racing southwards. In one week they advanced twice as far as they had in the previous seven, and could pass through Patton's newly constituted Third Army in a classic "leapfrog" of a pursuit force over a heavy breakthrough assault force.

Patton needed no urging. In a lightning but flexible armored thrust, comparable to any of the German drives of 1939-41, he pushed his men 150 miles south to the river Loire, trapping several enemy divisions. Then he lunged east to assist the encirclement of over 100,000 retreating Germans in the Falaise Pocket, and onwards north to the Seine crossings on both sides of Paris. The advance was so fast that it had to be resupplied by air drops. Not stopping on the Seine, Patton continued a total of some 350 miles east from Normandy to the fortress of Metz on the river Moselle. There, on 30th August, his spearhead finally bogged down in the fields around Gravelotte where the Prussian attack had also been temporarily blocked in 1870. Quite apart from the enemy's stiffening resistance, he was furious to learn that his Third army had now been allocated a low priority for resupply, so to sustain it he determined to rely on a mixture of hand-to-mouth logistic improvisations and subterfuges. These included the capture of considerable stocks of fuel from the enemy – not to mention from General Courtney H. Hodges' temptingly nearby First Army.

Patton was as brilliant at self publicity as he was at armored warfare, and he exploited the public's craving for an American military hero to set beside the Germans' Rommel and Guderian. As Bradley's former chief, moreover, he enjoyed more of that officer's favor than did Bradley's somewhat shy former subordinate, Hodges. Hodges was now nevertheless Patton's hierarchical equal, and as a skilled military technician he ultimately made a more solid contribution to the liberation of France. His men bore the brunt of the fighting in the pursuit around

ABOVE

*Two views from a landing craft bringing follow-up troops across the Normandy beaches to join the long files of men already making their way inland.*

Falaise; they actually liberated Paris itself, and set up the famous "Redball Express" – a continuous fast convoy of supply trucks running from Normandy to Paris. The First Army went on to create a new pocket at Mons in Belgium, where five more enemy divisions were captured. Meanwhile, on the seaward flank the British and Canadians were also very active – rushing forward to reach Brussels by 3rd September, and systematically opening the tenaciously-defended Channel ports. For all his brilliance, therefore, Patton's achievement during this period can scarcely be termed unique.

It was at this time that ugly national jealousies and personality clashes rose to the surface, centered mainly on Montgomery. The British Field Marshal had enjoyed overall tactical command in the Normandy battle, but was often criticized for his slow progress and plodding style. The American generals would naturally have preferred to run their own campaign, especially when their troop build-up was starting to give them a four to one numerical advantage over the British in France. They were therefore delighted to use a major reorganization at the end of July to achieve hierarchical parity with Montgomery.

Bradley now took command of 12th US Army Group, which included Patton's Third and Hodge's First Army, and would soon be joined by William H. Simpson's Ninth Army as it was formed in Normandy, followed a few months later by L. T. Gerow's Fifteenth Army. Advancing from Operation "Anvil" in the south of France, Patch's Seventh Army and the French First Army would be formed into General Jacob L. Devers' 6th Army Group. Meanwhile, the British and Canadian armies became 21st Army Group, which Montgomery would command, under Eisenhower, on an equal basis to Bradley in 12th Army Group and Devers in 6th. It thus appeared that Montgomery's influence had been curbed; but during the race through France he contrived to enrage the American generals still further by insisting on priority treatment for his British Second Army.

In this campaign the relative scarcity of operable ports meant there was a shortage of supplies. Eisenhower complained, for example, that some 8,000,000 mortar and artillery rounds were being consumed each month – or almost the same number as the AEF had used in the whole of the First World War. This in turn meant that a

major thrust by only one army could be fully supported logistically, so it was vital to know just which army should be selected for the honor. At first Montgomery argued that the British were best placed to win strategic dividends by advancing on a narrow front as close as possible to allied bases along the coast. Bradley and Patton, however, wanted to spread the supplies more widely so that they, too, could get a share of the action. Eisenhower therefore diluted the "narrow front" plan into a "broad front" attack that perhaps squandered the chance to end the war before Christmas.

In the event Montgomery went ahead with Operation "Market Garden"; a scaled-down version of his original narrow front advance through Holland and into the North German plain. The plan was for airborne forces to seize key bridges across the canals and rivers at Eindhoven, Grave, Nijmegen and Arnhem, all on 17th September. Ground forces would then race through to relieve the bridgeheads within 72 hours, consolidating the corridor. It was a bold conception that nearly succeeded. 101st Airborne Division achieved its objectives around Eindhoven while 82nd Airborne Division, although unable to

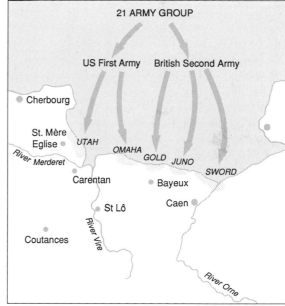

**THE NORMANDY LANDINGS**

*Members of a Navy beach battalion dig themselves into the edge of the dunes for their first night in Normandy. On succeeding days they would help manage the smooth flow of supplies from the sea into the battle.*

capture the Nijmegen bridge, did enable the British XXX Corps to do so when it arrived overland. In a week's successful fighting there would be some 3,700 US casualties. Arnhem itself, however, turned out to be the "bridge too far" that the 11,000 men of First British Airborne Division could not secure. Instead, they were thrown on the defensive by panzer counter-attacks, and could not be relieved by XXX Corps in time. They had to be evacuated with some 80 percent losses, and the final drive into Germany was postponed for several months.

After the Arnhem failure the allies realized they were over extended. They needed to open more port facilities and pause to draw breath for the next push. This would be across the Siegfried Line, or West Wall, that ran the whole length of the German border. Although not a very imposing fortification when it had first been built before the war, it was now being extensively improved and reinforced. It ran through some very difficult forest terrain, and in places could be strengthened by inundations, if the Germans blew certain key dams. Its outworks at Metz were also very strong, and it would be 22nd November before Patton could capture the city in badly deteriorating weather. He reached the main Siegfried position only in mid-December, supported on his right flank by more dramatic advances by Devers' 6th Army Group.

Along most of the rest of the front there was inaction and regrouping, but Hodges' First Army tried to beat a path through the Siegfried Line on a very narrow frontage – and with a shortage of artillery ammunition – in the area of Aachen. The city was captured only on 21st October after savage house to house combat. Then in November Hodges and Simpson together renewed the advance through the muddy Hurtgen forest and towards the strategic Roer dams. The Germans were in no sense taken by surprise. They had staked out a depth defense that made this battle, in Ernest Hemingway's vivid phrase, like "Passchendaele with tree bursts." Casualties mounted horrifically, reaching no less than 85,000 for the whole operation around Aachen from the start of October. Neither the bogged armor nor the shell-deprived artillery could offer any relief, until progress was finally halted by the German threat to blow the Roer dams at Schmidt, following the US failure to capture them. It was realized that a whole new operation would be needed to take this objective. As at Arnhem and Metz, in fact, the thrust past Aachen turned into another allied failure that might have been avoided if only there had been a greater concentration of effort at one single point, rather than three separate lunges at different places.

On the German side, however, there was now to be an equal and compensating fault of strategy

*Reinforcement infantry comes ashore towards the end of the Normandy battle.*

*Paratroops patrolling St. Mère Église to clear the area of German snipers. Since the airborne soldiers were very widely dispersed on landing, they often found themselves interspersed with enemy soldiers.*

*Eisenhower stresses the need for "full victory" to 101st Airborne Division "Screaming Eagles" just prior to the Normandy assault. Together with 82nd Airborne Division, these forces had to secure the area around "Utah" Beach to facilitate the amphibious landings.*

in the shape of Hitler's desperate last fling through the Ardennes. Unknown to the allies, he had husbanded a powerful armored striking force of over eight army corps, and had secretly assembled it opposite a fifty-mile stretch of Bradley's front line. The attack sector was certainly well chosen, being held by little more than Middleton's VIII Corps, convalescing from hard fighting in Brittany, and some elements of Gerow's V Corps, fresh from Hurtgen forest. But, as was usual with Hitler, the plan was far too grandiose. Instead of using his advantage to shake the allied campaign locally and then strengthen the defenses of the Reich, as his generals would have preferred, he insisted on trying to burst all the way through the Ardennes forest and on to Antwerp, a hundred miles from the start line. In this way he hoped to split Eisenhower's forces in two and end the war in the west, just as he had done in 1940 on very much the same ground. He failed to realize that warfare in 1944 was no longer fought by the same rules as in 1940, because even if the commanding allied air forces could be grounded by bad weather, this would still not neutralize the commanding allied mechanized forces on the ground.

In 1940 the Germans had passed through the Ardennes before they had to fight; but in 1944 they were resisted every inch of the way. Despite

being outnumbered four to one, Middleton's troops almost halted the green *Volksgrenadier* divisions that were sent against them during the short cold day of 16th December. There was widespread panic in US rear areas when it was learned that German commandos dressed as Americans were roaming loose with murder and mayhem in their hearts – but this mood barely affected either the front line soldiers or the higher levels of command. When viewed from the map boards of higher headquarters, the crisis soon began to look perfectly containable, even if it had initially come as a nasty surprise. By 17th December numerous flanking formations were already being calmly shifted into position along the flanks of the growing enemy salient. Collins' VII Corps, Ridgway's XVIII Airborne Corps and the British XXX Corps took up their positions along the northern flank, while Patton's Third Army prepared a powerful counter-attack from the south.

The Germans soon found they were caught in a gigantic trap. They were unable to reach even their intermediate objective at Dinant on the river Meuse, let alone their "port too far" at Antwerp. Precisely the bad weather and forest cover that they had deliberately chosen as a defense against allied air attack also proved to be a major hindrance to forward movement. The Ardennes forest loomed as murky, wet and constricting to Hitler's spearheads as had the Hurtgen forest to Hodges' the month before. By the same token the inconspicuous rearward stockpiling of fuel, that had helped the Germans achieve the initial strategic surprise, became a major liability as soon as their mechanized spearheads started to run ahead. Unlike France in 1940, there were no wayside gas stations that could top up the panzers when they began to run dry. Nor could American resistance within the salient be suppressed. At the key communications node of Bastogne the spirited defense by 101st Airborne Division – both physical and verbal – provided an efficient dampener to Nazi ambitions.

The turning point in the battle came on 23rd December, when a change in the weather allowed flying to be resumed. Bastogne could be resupplied by air and – far more significantly – a massive interdiction bombing campaign could be launched against the enemy's lines of supply. On 26th December Patton's 4th Armored Division smashed through to Bastogne itself and, although this led to more than a week of frenetic German counter-attacks ordered directly by Hitler, it really marked the beginning of the end of this battle.

Montgomery had been given command of all Bradley's forces north of the "Bulge" – despite the protests of many American commanders – and he began his attack on 3rd January 1945. By 16th January he had reclaimed most of the Ardennes

RIGHT

*Elmer Habbs, native of Delaware and member of the 82nd Airborne Division, relaxes outside the town his outfit captured the night before the seaborne invasion, then held tenaciously. Fortunately for the American paratroops, their drop zone had been changed at the last moment when an enemy division was identified in their original target area.*

## THE RHINELAND

and linked hands with Patton. By the end of February the allies had more than restored the line of 16 December. German losses were very great – almost 200,000 men and 1,400 tanks or assault guns – although they were never "pocketed" except in a relatively small French afterthought operation around Colmar at the start of February. The Americans suffered some 76,000 casualties, so it was scarcely a cheap victory. The difference was that Hitler could not afford such losses at this stage in the war, whereas the allied program for the assault on Germany was merely delayed by six weeks.

A new round of offensives began on 8th February, in the Nijmegen area and at the Roer dams. Since the latter could be seized by V Corps only after the Germans had opened them, they delayed further operations lower down the river for two weeks. On 25th February, however, there was a general assault all along the line, and enemy resistance west of the Rhine was soon in ruins. By 10th March the allies had reached the great river along its whole length between Nijmegen and Coblenz and – best of all – they had captured an intact bridge.

On 7th March leading elements of 9th US Armored Division had entered the small town of Remagen, about fifteen miles upstream from Bonn. They saw the railroad bridge still standing, but heard from a prisoner that it was soon due to be blown. Racing forward, they managed to tear up the demolition wires and secure the far side before the main charges could go up. This was one of those very rare platoon actions that have huge strategic consequences, since it fortuitously solved a problem that had been troubling Bradley for some time. In the February fighting he had been forced to concede priority to Montgomery on his left flank, and now he was being asked to send troops to help the French on the right. He was frustrated that the final campaign of the war would not, apparently, be spearheaded by Americans. When the capture of the Remagen bridge was reported to him by Hodges, therefore, Bradley was elated and exclaimed "Hot dog, Courtney, this will blow him wide open!" It gave him the lever he needed to reverse the original plan and start a major US offensive right through the center of the German line, consigning the British and French alike to a more secondary role.

Instead of only a main British Rhine crossing aimed around the northern flank of the Ruhr industrial area, there would now also be a still greater US thrust around the south, making a double envelopment. Before this took place, however, Patton was unleashed into the Rhineland between Coblenz and Strasbourg, to extend the start line and finally round up the enemy being driven by Devers' 6th Army Group. Some quarter of a million prisoners were captured between the

11th and 21st March, for the loss of around 12,000 US casualties. Two further bridgeheads over the Rhine were also seized, at Oppenheim and Boppard. Meanwhile, Montgomery made a crossing on a broad front around Wesel on 23rd March, and the great encirclement of the Ruhr was under way.

Resistance was patchy, since for every Hitler Youth determined to make a last ditch stand there were a hundred dispirited under- or over-age *Volksgrenadiers* only too ready to surrender to the Americans rather than to the Russians. Eisenhower's spearheads reached the river Elbe and the Czech frontier by the middle of April, linking on the 25th with Russian soldiers coming from the east. As the advance continued, however, the joy of victory was tainted by the horrific evidence of Nazi genocide uncovered along the way. Images of Belsen, Buchenwald and Dachau came to overshadow the way this whole war would be remembered forever afterwards, just as the Hiroshima bomb became the most emotive symbol of the war against Japan.

Victory in Europe was finally won when the Red Army sacked Berlin, employing some 6,000 tanks and 25,000 artillery pieces, and at a cost of 100,000 casualties within a week. Despite warnings from London about the likely long term future in this zone, Eisenhower had been happy to keep US forces well out of the bloodbath. He was content to share in the general relief at Hitler's suicide on 30th April, followed by unconditional surrender on 7th May. It had been a long, hard road from Operation "Torch" through Italy and Normandy to the very heart of the Reich; but it had ultimately led to total victory and the overthrow of Nazism. The effort and losses of those three years certainly established the USA as a dominant power in Europe, in a way that Pershing's campaign in 1918 had not; but it also did far more – it restored freedom to many Western nations. The war, in short, had been very well worth fighting.

### ABOVE LEFT

*Firing a mortar from the Normandy dunes. The unconcerned appearance of onlookers suggests that this is not "in anger," and there is no risk of return fire.*

### LEFT

*The first successful thrust out of the "Utah" beachhead struck northwest to Cherbourg. Here some of the spearhead infantry move down a track near Valognes where a cyclist unit – perhaps itself American – has obviously been badly handled. Note the short fields of fire in the hedgerow country – a major tactical difficulty for the attacker throughout the Normandy theater.*

A French cyclist displays his gratitude to the American spearheads forging south from the Normandy breakout in Operation Cobra. This is Rennes, the capital of Brittany, badly shattered by allied bombing.

The fruits of victory. A Norman farmer and his wife welcome their liberators with a suitable libation.

US Sherman tanks rumble through La Lavandau near Toulon, southern France, in Operation Anvil (later called "Dragoon") at the end of August 1944. This operation secured good port facilities far quicker than the attack through Normandy, but it has been criticized for weakening the offensive in Italy and diverting resources from the thrust to the Rhine in northern France.

*US airborne soldiers advancing through Holland as part of Operation Market Garden, September 1944.*

FAR LEFT

*Rejoicings in liberated Paris, France, as French, American and British troops, with a bewildering miscellany of uniforms and vehicles, attempt to push through the enthusiastic crowds. The scene is outside the Paris town hall, 30th August 1944.*

LEFT

*Each of these self-propelled 105 mm howitzers fired some 500 shells against German positions in the village of Samree, on the road to Houffallize, during the US counter-attack to clear "the Bulge" in the Ardennes forest, mid-January 1945. Obviously the allied armies were caught out by the snowy weather, since they have not converted to white camouflage schemes.*

**ABOVE**

US troops patrolling the war-torn town of Laroche during the Allies' Ardennes counter-offensive. Note the steep wooded slopes behind the town, of the sort which helped give this area its misleading reputation of being "impassable" to armored forces.

**LEFT**

The Ludendorff railroad bridge at Remagen, near Bonn, was fortuitously captured by the reconnaissance troops of Lieutenant General H. Hodges' US 1st Army, over two weeks before the master plan called for a Rhine crossing. This had the effect of channeling resources unexpectedly to the south of the Ruhr, and may not have led to any overall saving in time.

*Lieutenant General William H. Simpson's US 9th Army brings up pontoons for its Rhine crossings near Düsseldorf on the night of 23rd-24th March 1945. The operation had been severely delayed by the ever-cautious Montgomery, much to American chagrin.*

*Lieutenant General Alexander Patch's US 7th Army crosses the Rhine at high speed, hard on the heels of Patton's 3rd Army, just south of Worms on 28th March 1945.*

ABOVE LEFT

*Crossing the Rhine in an assault boat with "the lead flying around like hail," as one participant described it.*

ABOVE

*Men of the 7th Army celebrate their victory from the dais at Nürnberg from which Hitler used to address his rallies. The city had been captured only after a stiff fight, and it was feared that still more frenzied last-ditch resistance would be encountered in the Nazis' "national redoubt" around Berchtesgaden, just east of Munich.*

LEFT

*A Rhine bridge briskly established by Patton's 3rd Army in the area of Mainz.*

RIGHT

*The "down side" of victory in Germany was the discovery of evidence testifying to the most horrific Nazi crimes. Here the bodies of some 700 slave laborers are uncovered, massacred before the liberation army could reach them, at Gardelegen on the road to Berlin.*

US and Soviet co-belligerents join hands as their thrusts deep into Germany, from West and East respectively, meet up at Apollensdorf. The first meetings had taken place on 25th April 1945.

RIGHT

V-E Day in London, 7th May 1945. An American soldier reads of German surrender in a British newspaper.

FAR RIGHT

The 86th Infantry Division returns home rejoicing to New York, waving flags taken from their defeated foe.

# CHAPTER SIX

# "There is No Substitute for Victory!"

*The Korean War, 1950-3*

The problem with victory in WWII was that it came in two separate parts. Whereas the Western allies achieved very much the type of settlement that they had fought for in the West, the Russians made sure that they secured a very different type of victory in the East. Both blocs doubtless deserved to achieve their dearest ambitions in return for their many bitter sacrifices – but the unfortunate fact was that these ambitions were often incompatible. Whereas the West had originally gone to war to preserve the independence of Poland, the USSR had always wanted to annexe that country. Whereas the Western aim was to rehabilitate and re-civilize Germany, the Red Army had merely wished to dominate and plunder her. Whereas Roosevelt had wanted to achieve a better world through his "Four Freedoms," Stalin had pursued a more "secure" world for himself and his cronies through mass murder and mass conquest. Whereas America had fought for free trade and the United Nations, Russia had fought for state centralism and the Communist International.

*Berlin was a divided city from its occupation by the Allies in 1945 until the destruction of the Berlin Wall at the end of 1989. Here US and Soviet patrols eye each other over the demarkation line on Potsdamer Platz in August 1948, the spot at which a senior American official had just been arrested and detained for 21 hours by Russian police.*

*Tempelhof Airport just after the epic 1948-9 airlift that saved Berlin. At its peak, up to 927 aircraft per day flew supplies into the beleaguered city. Representing the limited use of military forces short of open fighting, the operation symbolized the political complexity that would make the Cold War so baffling to many Americans.*

"Cold War" was the almost inevitable result of this fracture between the underlying aims of East and West; nor could its continuing "coldness" always be taken for granted. As early as 1948 Stalin's blockade of West Berlin very nearly led to direct hostilities between the two sides, when USAF General Hoyt Vandenberg urged President Harry S. Truman to relieve the beleaguered city by a thrust with armored forces. The Berlin commander, US General Lucius Clay, also had contingency plans for fighting such a war – although Truman fortunately sidestepped the issue by ordering an airlift that avoided confrontations on the ground. If there had been serious fighting it would surely have escalated rapidly above the nuclear threshold, since western conventional forces at this time were so hopelessly outnumbered by the Soviets. Indeed, it is even questionable whether the limited stockpile of atomic weapons then available to the Americans would have been adequate to halt a concerted Soviet tank attack. Russian military doctrine was still officially dismissive of the nuclear threat on the tactical battlefield, and in the conditions of the late 1940s probably quite rightly so. It was one thing to vaporise the mass of humanity packed helplessly in the center of an immobile city; but it was an altogether different proposition to attempt to take out the armored soldiers of a tank army moving fast and tactically dispersed, across some 25,000 square kilometers of undulating terrain. In 1948 there could be no clear certainty of victory for either side, hence no very pressing desire to start a war. The age of mutual deterrence, in other words, had already begun.

For all that, the USA did actually fight and win at least one small "hot war" against the communists during 1947-9: in Greece. This US commitment, the very first to be envisaged by the famous Marshall Plan of 1947, represented a firm assertion of the 1945 Yalta agreement that Greece should fall within the Western sphere of influence. There had been a power struggle between rival resistance forces that had started at the moment of liberation in 1944, so the Americans now sent arms and advisers to the royalist side. This had the effect of provoking the communists into launching a final, all-out assault. Perhaps predictably, it was the most dangerous thing for the health of their own supporters that the communists could possibly have done, and their movement was quickly crushed in frontal battles, with heavy casualties. In the USA itself, however, there were to be two unfortunate long term results of this experience. Among the military it taught the misleading lesson that the art of counter-insurgency was just a matter of throwing conventional arms, troops and money at the problem, to produce a quick victory that cut through the apparently baffling complexities of

*The initial United Nations deployment to defend South Korea was unable to save the capital, Seoul; but during July 1950 hastily assembled troops were able to secure a perimeter around Pusan on the southern coast. This would be the only United Nations-sponsored war before the 1991 Gulf War.*

*US troops laying telephone wire as they move up to the front, August 1950. Meanwhile, South Korean civilians flee from the fierce northern assault.*

The biggest anti-communist war of this era, however, was the United Nations' 1950 intervention to reverse the occupation of South Korea by the North. The invasion had started on 25th June, but the first trickle of US reinforcements was already starting to arrive on the 29th, commanded – for the UN – by General Douglas MacArthur. Fighting a series of heroic delaying actions alongside Republic of Korea (ROK) units, they fell back gradually throughout July to a perimeter along the Naktong river, covering the port of Pusan. Here they fought a bitter defensive battle throughout August and early September, with inadequate troops or equipment to hold the 130 miles of front in force at every point. General Walton H. Walker's Eighth Army headquarters therefore had to exploit mobility and tactical flexibility to the maximum, improvising with whatever was on hand as each new crisis arose. Sometimes he was unlucky, and a number of UN units were overrun as the perimeter shrank. On the whole, however, the position was held and

"hearts and minds." This assumption would later have some very damaging consequences when applied to Vietnam, especially after the Korean War had seemed to teach that Asian communism could be defeated by conventional military defense rather than by a mix of police, social and political programs.

A second postwar counter-insurgency victory would also be won between 1949 and 1955 in the newly-independent Philippines, which had just lost an estimated million lives as a result of WWII – over three times as many as were lost to the USA in that conflict, and almost exactly the same number that would later be lost by the Vietnamese during the Second Indochina War. In the light of these sacrifices many of the anti-Japanese Filipino guerrillas had understandably hoped for a more enlightened and economically advantageous government after the war; but in the event they felt themselves to have been badly let down. They therefore reverted to guerrilla resistance against their former sponsors, turning to communism as a better hope. Their misfortune was that they eventually came up against President Ramon Magsaysay, a rare strong man who knew just how to mix together a judicious war-winning brew of lavish US aid, military counter-insurgency, economic reform and social justice. Once again, therefore, the United States found herself coming out almost effortlessly on the winning side of a bitter counter-insurgency campaign. She drew the misleading conclusion that aid to in-place native hierarchies would automatically prove to be cost-effective. Unfortunately, it would take many years of South Vietnamese government corruption to persuade her that this was not always automatically the case.

*To break the Pusan deadlock, General MacArthur exploited the flexibility of amphibious forces by mounting a daring assault from the sea against the enemy's rear, Inchon 15th September 1950. Here marines swarm over the side of an assault ship to man landing craft for the final journey to the beach.*

*A US 75 mm recoilless anti tank rifle awaits the arrival of North Korean armor before the Pusan perimeter. In this war the American forces were often outnumbered by the enemy, but they normally enjoyed a considerable "combat multiplier" in the form of plentiful modern weaponry. Note also the M3A1 .45 cal. "grease gun."*

the ferocity of the North Korean assault melted away. The UN air forces had quickly achieved total command of the skies, and were now hammering hard against the enemy's lines of communication.

While Walker was holding the line on the ground, MacArthur was preparing a bold counter-blow that would prove to be decisive. Instead of merely reinforcing the hard-pressed garrison of Pusan, he would use the "indirect approach" by making an amphibious landing in the enemy's rear. The ROK capital, Seoul, was identified as a key focus in the North Korean logistic chain, and MacArthur wanted to seize it by a blow through the port of Inchon. This was a shrewd decision that achieved surprise, since the complex channels and tidal patterns at Inchon made it a difficult and unlikely place to land. There was also a feint towards Kunsan, nearer to Pusan, designed to keep the enemy guessing. Then on 15th September the US X Corps started to come ashore, led by 1st Marine Division. Opposition was light, and the nearby airfield was made operational within two days. However, it took most of the remainder of the month to fight through the streets of Seoul itself as resistance stiffened.

**KOREA**

TOP

*Men of the 1st US Marine Division cross the sea wall at Inchon before thrusting deep inland. The site had been carefully chosen to achieve maximum surprise.*

ABOVE

*Mopping up North Korean resistance in the Inchon area, as MacArthur's offensive swings into gear to "cut off and kill" the communist army.*

Meanwhile the Eighth Army was breaking out of the Pusan perimeter, and by 26th September its spearhead had joined hands with X Corps. This closed the trap behind most of the invading northern army, which now rapidly fell apart. The communist forces degenerated into a disorganized *sauve qui peut* to recross the 38th Parallel in small groups, often wearing civilian dress. Some of these groups began to fight as guerrillas behind UN lines, but in general co-ordinated resistance within South Korea was at an end.

It was at this point that MacArthur asked to be authorized to continue the pursuit north of the 38th Parallel, in support of ROK ambitions to reunite the two Koreas and also in pursuance of his military orders to destroy the enemy army. Some UN members believed this policy amounted to an act of aggression, and withdrew their support; but the General Assembly approved it on 6th October. The forces of some 23 member nations continued to participate in the battle. Despite considerable disorganization and logistic shortfalls as MacArthur restructured his forces, therefore, the pursuit continued northwards. Pyongyang was captured on 20th October, while an ambitious parachute drop by 187th Airborne

Regimental Combat Team leapfrogged forward of the front line. The ROK 6th Division reached the Chinese border along the Yalu river on 26th October, followed by belated amphibious landings on the east coast by X Corps.

It was now revealed that the UN forces had been over optimistic in assessing the threat from China, whose repeated warnings against the invasion had been disregarded. Not even after Chinese ambushes were encountered from 25th October onwards did UN intelligence analysts initially believe they signalled a major strategic counter attack. MacArthur was prohibited from flying aircraft over Chinese territory north of the Yalu, so was deprived of a major source of reconnaissance. In any case, the Chinese units were superbly concealed and camouflaged, which led to very great underestimates of their true numbers. Nor were they seen as very tactically threatening, since they were badly short of battlefield communications and heavy weapons, preferring obsolete close quarter charges to more sophisticated fighting methods. Apart from the initial rout of ROK II Corps and 8th US Cavalry Regiment, and some other local surprises, the allies for a time even seemed to be getting the

better of the engagements. South of Chosin reservoir, for example, ROK forces and US marines mauled a Chinese division. Nevertheless, the allied advance to the Yalu had not been properly phased or resupplied, and its unity of command was fractured down the center by rough country between the Eighth Army to the west and X Corps to the east. Its spearheads were therefore vulnerable and widely dispersed unless they halted to regroup. MacArthur would not wait for this, however, but took success in the early clashes as evidence that he could still press forward regardless.

The Chinese storm finally burst in earnest on 25 November, definitively dispersing the ROK II Corps, badly damaging the US 2nd Division and outflanking the Eighth Army from the east. There was severe fighting as Walker struggled to disentangle his forces first from the Chongchon river line, then from the hills south of Pyongyang and finally back to the 38th Parallel – a total retreat of some 200 miles within three weeks. Walker himself was killed in a jeep accident very soon afterwards, and was replaced in command by General Matthew B. Ridgway, formerly a leading pioneer of US airborne operations during WWII.

Meanwhile at "Frozen Chosin" General Oliver Smith's 1st Marine Division found itself surrounded by some seven enemy divisions. Temperatures fell as low as 20° below, which was cold enough to burst open a rocket launcher round or to seize up an automatic weapon. The men certainly came to see the point of Genghis Khan's dictum that "No one fights in the lands of the Mongols in wintertime." Nevertheless, they did indeed fight their way gallantly out of the trap, drawing supplies and tactical support from the air and rescuing some 14,000 men for a cost of about 4,000 casualties. They had also inflicted enormous losses on the enemy before being expertly evacuated by sea to take their place in the Eighth Army line.

The Chinese were not slow to close up on the 38th Parallel, which they assailed by almost half a million men on 1st January 1951. Still groggy from the longest retreat in American military history, the 300,000 defenders buckled under the blow and began to fall back towards the south, evacuating Seoul. Continuous air strikes

LEFT

*LSTs beached at low tide at Inchon, as they disgorge streams of vehicles and supplies to feed the UN battle line. Such scenes had been very familiar in WWII, and Uncle Sam still retained the equipment and expertise needed to reproduce them in Cold War operations. On this occasion the planning time was far shorter than normal, yet the operation was a complete success.*

nevertheless harassed the pursuing Chinese forces, which encountered serious logistic difficulties and had lost all forward impetus by the middle of January. Ridgway was able to consolidate a line about 50 miles south of Seoul, and even go over to the counter attack.

Three months of fluid fighting followed, in which the ground lost since 1st January was recaptured. Seoul itself was reoccupied on 14th March, and by mid-April a strong defensive line had been staked out just to the north of the 38th Parallel. The spring thaw was imposing major obstacles to movement, but it served to delay communist regrouping more than that of the UN. It was only in the last week of April that the Chinese were able to launch a new attack. This made a 20-mile bound forward but suffered very heavy casualties and failed to capture Seoul. Some ROK formations were shattered, but in general the allies had by now taken the measure of their opponents, and were often claiming to exchange casualties at a rate approaching ten Chinese to every one UN. By early June the April line had been restored and the enemy was starting to make peace feelers. After a year of see-saw movements across the 38th Parallel, it seemed as though the war was finally entering a more static and politically containable phase.

Meanwhile, another major indication of this change in mood had been seen when MacArthur was dismissed by President Truman on 11th April. The general had been anxious to avenge his earlier defeats by expanding the war into China, especially by bombing the Manchurian sanctuaries that had been so frustratingly off limits during the November and December fighting. He wanted to use nuclear explosives to seal off the Yalu river line, and Chinese Nationalist forces from Taiwan to invade the mainland. The president, however, saw these policies as unduly provocative to the Russians, who might retaliate by launching military action in Europe – now alarmingly denuded of Western troops due to the war in Korea. From his higher political vantage point, therefore, Truman saw a need to dampen down the war, not to expand it. He removed the invasion of North Korea from the agenda, and continued to impose geographical limits to action in order to avoid the risk of an accidental start to another world war. When MacArthur made his dissatisfaction public, he was replaced as UN commander by Ridgway, who was in turn replaced in the Eighth Army by General James A. Van Fleet.

MacArthur's dismissal marked a turning point not only in the Korean war itself, but also in the whole history of warfare. It signalled the start of an era of "limited" or local wars, in which all-out military action was increasingly circumscribed by the political requirements of the central Cold

TOP

*MacArthur's push from Inchon led him into a controversial advance through North Korea to the Yalu River frontier with China. This provoked a surprise Chinese intervention from the end of October, and a bitter winter campaign.*

ABOVE

*The retreat from the Yalu was well handled despite repeated enemy attacks, but it still represented the longest retreat in American military history. A solid defensive line was finally established only to the south of Seoul.*

LEFT

*Men of the 1st US Cavalry Division, without their mounts.*

dug in deep and continuously "improved their positions." The UN eventually established command of the much-disputed "Punchbowl" and "Iron Triangle" areas; but beyond these lay inhospitable mountain regions that were powerfully fortified by the enemy. Local operations spluttered on while the armistice conference explored the possibilities for peace, first at Kaesong and then at Panmunjom.

In 1952 there was no large scale fighting, but continuing patrol activity. Meanwhile, the communists reinforced their front both quantitatively and qualitatively. They almost achieved a numerical superiority of three to one over the UN force of 300,000 men, and now greatly enhanced their combat power with large numbers of Russian field guns, anti-aircraft guns and aircraft. From its traditional structure as a weapon of mass guerrilla warfare, the People's Liberation Army now became more technological and more hierarchically organized, although it could never

War balance – a balance that was now being underwritten on both sides by growing stockpiles of nuclear weapons. When MacArthur declared "There is no substitute for victory!" he was therefore expressing an outdated military ideal. He was still living in the ideals of WWII, when the aim had been to force the enemy's unconditional surrender by the use of every available means. Truman, by contrast, knew that international stability and the avoidance of nuclear war was a higher goal than local victory, even if it meant pulling punches or letting the enemy off the hook. It was in the essence of limited war that one should be prepared to accept defeat if necessary, since wars in which defeat was unacceptable were by definition no longer limited.

After the Chinese failure to break through in May, the intensity of fighting died down. The UN was experiencing ammunition shortages, and the Monsoon combined with White House caution to bog down offensive operations. For many months the front line scarcely moved, although both sides

RIGHT

*Fighting for Hill 400 on the last day of 1951. By this time General Matthew B. Ridgway had restored "balance" to the UN line, although this often led to heavy positional fighting reminiscent of the trenches in WWI. Political restraints prevented any widening of the war, which was frustrating to GIs on the ground.*

seriously downgrade allied command of the air.

Armistice negotiations continued into 1953, supported by a sharp escalation of communist pressure on the battlefield during the spring of that year. In actions such as the famous battle of Pork Chop Hill, essentially barren pieces of real estate changed hands backwards and forwards in fierce trench warfare that everyone knew was little more than a cosmetic backdrop for the diplomatic negotiations – but none the less deadly for that. In an ominous foretaste of more recent hostage-taking episodes the Panmanjom negotiations came to revolve largely around issues connected with the return of prisoners. It was soon revealed how many of those held by the communists had been tortured or "brain washed," with almost 60 percent of American prisoners dying of disease or being killed in captivity. This marked a contrast with the very widespread reluctance of communist prisoners to be returned to their countries of origin. Some prison camp riots were nevertheless engineered by North Korean agitators, leading to several hundred casualties when UN troops restored order. The whole problem looked highly intractable, although Stalin's death and the election of President Eisenhower eventually combined to change the international political climate. The ceasefire was finally signed on 27th July, although talks to find a permanent peace continue at Panmunjom to this very day.

Altogether approximately 40,000 Americans were killed in Korea, and a further 100,000 were wounded, missing or taken prisoner. In just three years, therefore, the "butcher's bill" was very comparable to that of the much longer Vietnam involvement during the 1960s and '70s. Korean and Chinese losses were also comparably high, with a total of some two million battle casualties and a further four million military and civilian deaths connected with the war. For all its political "limitations," therefore, this was still a very high intensity conflict that only went to prove that the Cold War could be very dangerous indeed.

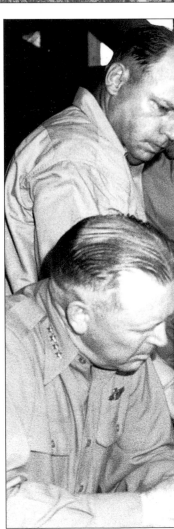

RIGHT

*Master Sergeant Francis Connors of Bayonne, NJ, extracts himself after raising the flag on an exposed position at "Sandbag Castle," as trench warfare continued into January 1953. Chinese infantry were firing at him from a range of just 15 yards.*

*Three North American F-86D Sabre jets on an early exercise in California. As the only available single-seat interceptor, they played a vital role in combatting Chinese Mig 15s in the skies over Korea. By the end of the war they were claiming 13 Mig kills for each Sabre shot down in air-to-air combat.*

*Combining diplomacy with warfare, United Nations negotiators press for a ceasefire at the Panmunjom talks while the biggest offensive for two years begins on the battlefield, 16th July 1953.*

*General Mark W. Clark, who succeeded Ridgway as UN commander, signs the armistice at Munsan Truce Camp, 29th July 1953. The exchange of POW's was a major difficulty throughout the negotiations, since so many UN prisoners had been murdered and ill-treated by the communists, yet so few communist prisoners wished to be repatriated.*

# CHAPTER SEVEN

# THE NAM (1)

*From advisory teams to the biggest hi-tech war since WWII, 1959-68*

The Korean war of 1950-3 had been fought with essentially the same technology as the battle for Normandy in 1944. Large masses of well coordinated field artillery pounded the enemy trenches as tank-infantry teams made short bounds forward or conducted integrated trench warfare defenses. Allied air superiority provided heavy interdiction strikes against the enemy's line of communication, while naval gunfire scoured all his installations within range. Admittedly, there were some promising technical innovations just beginning to make their presence felt, such as the widespread use of jet aircraft on both sides; routine use of helicopters; and even a proliferation of flak jackets. Nevertheless, in the early 1950s these weapons could not radically change the general shape of warfare. The only really significant technical novelty was the introduction of battlefield nuclear weapons, designed to raise the level of deterrence and make up for NATO's inferiority in manpower numbers. Yet not even these could always be taken entirely seriously – for example the Davy Crockett mortar had a lethal radius that exceeded its range. In the early 1980s a former US secretary of defense confessed that he would never have contemplated the use of tactical nuclear weapons under any possible foreseeable set of circumstances.

*One of the great turning points in the Cold War: Fidel Castro enters Havana in triumph on 8th January 1959, at the head of a ragged guerrilla band. Against all expectations, he would soon establish a communist foothold "behind American lines" every bit as significant as the West's Berlin foothold within the Eastern camp.*

*Castro's revolution provoked a violent anti-Castro reaction among Cuban exiles supported by the USA. Here an armed detachment plans the Bay of Pigs invasion that would be launched forty-eight hours later on 17th April 1961.*

It was predicted that the next war for Germany would look depressingly similar to the last one – apart from a startling change-round of allies and enemies as the new (1949) NATO Alliance squared up to the still newer (1955) Warsaw Pact. In the event these gloomy prospects did in fact mean that the potential aggressor in Europe was suitably deterred – although the same reasoning would also work in reverse with equal power when NATO was deterred from intervening in the Hungarian uprising of 1956, and then in the Prague Spring of 1968.

Similar processes of deterrence also applied to the other US alliances that were now starting to ring the globe. In the Middle East the USA was able first to deter Britain and France from their Suez adventure of 1956, then to rally in support of her CENTO friends by limited deterrent deployments to Jordan in 1957 and to Lebanon in 1958 – all with a total loss of just one combat casualty. Within the framework of Southeast Asia's SEATO treaty the USA sent aid first to the French and then to the Diem governments in Vietnam; to the Philippines against their internal insurgency, and to Chiang Kai Shek in his confrontations with the mainland Chinese in Taiwan, Matsu and Quemoy.

By 1961 America appeared to have succeeded admirably in her role as "world policeman." She had ensured a fair degree of stability in the international scene, apart perhaps from Fidel Castro's Cuban revolution that the 1961 Bay of Pigs proxy war was unable to overthrow. In the following year, however, the damage even here seemed to have been largely reversed by President John F. Kennedy's resolute stand during the

ABOVE RIGHT

*Ernesto (Che) Guevara, veteran Cuban guerrilla-turned-Economic Minister, denounces the USA to the Organization of American States in Uruguay, August 1961. Che Guevara became a cult figure among radical intellectuals, but was hunted and shot on active service in Bolivia, 1968.*

RIGHT

*At the end of April 1965 the Dominican Republic had fallen into a state of civil war between two rival military juntas. US troops were deployed to defuse the situation, but were widely suspected of making merely a knee-jerk anti-communist reaction. During May, however, they helped establish a compromise caretaker régime supported by the Organization of American States. Pictured here is an arms search in the "constitutionalist" capital city, Santo Domingo.*

Missile Crisis. In January 1964 US troops could resist Castro-inspired rioting in the Panama Canal Zone – suffering some 88 casualties in exchange for up to 300 Panamanians. Then in late April and early May 1965 no less than 31,600 American soldiers and marines were lifted into the Dominican Republic to quell a revolt that had also been infiltrated by Castro supporters. This deployment would be maintained for a year, with a casualty list of some 200 Americans. During the remainder of the 1960s US advisers and military aid would also help bolster many other Latin American regimes against the Cuban challenge; the most famous incident coming in 1968, when Che Guevara was tracked down and killed by Bolivian rangers.

President Kennedy certainly inherited much from his predecessors, but he also brought a new wave of strategic thinking to the White House and to the Pentagon. Not only did he represent a younger generation that was unencumbered by decades of shouldering heavy responsibilities, but he also faced a quite novel set of strategic challenges. Since the Soviet Sputnik had been launched in 1957 the United States had for the first time been brought within range of a credible strategic threat. In response she had already started to go ahead with a hardened nuclear second strike capability and an awesome nuclear navy, but with Kennedy's election the creation of greatly improved ever-ready *conventional* forces was also given high priority. He saw that at a time when the two super powers would soon have complete nuclear parity with each other, there would be a

state of Mutually Assured Destruction ("MAD") whereby nuclear release could be justified only in the gravest of national emergencies. The ordinary conditions of locally-limited warfare would no longer include a credible place for nuclear weapons, as they had perhaps done during the generation of Truman and Eisenhower. Instead, Kennedy realized that most everyday military situations would in future have to be resolved at force levels below the nuclear threshold or, in the case of guerrilla or insurgency threats, even below the conventional threshold itself.

Kennedy was supported in his military re-think by his Secretary of Defense Robert McNamara, who brought hard financial cost-benefit analysis techniques to bear on military procurement programs and strategic concepts alike. He assessed that with the right investment the USA could soon build an ever-ready conventional capability sufficient to fight two Korean-size wars simultaneously, backed by specialist teams to support smaller scale counter-insurgency operations elsewhere. In an attempt to break free of the tradition by which US wars were usually hastily improvised affairs, he put a great deal of effort into improving permanently-available strategic lift capacity and general flexibility. By 1965 America therefore held a bright new sword in her hand that could be quickly projected to any point on the globe. It was made all the brighter by a multitude of glittering technical breakthroughs in fields such as guided weapons, electronics, satellite surveillance and communications – and especially helicopters.

A whole new age of military tactics seemed to be dawning, in which small but hard-hitting airmobile combat teams could perform all the tasks – and more – that would normally have needed unwieldy formations of fixed wing aircraft, artillery, armored cavalry and infantry. Instead of the heavy bludgeon of past wars, there would now be a light and elegant rapier. To build this new arm McNamara set up the "Howze Board" in 1962. Its brief was to make radical new recommendations for army aviation, including tactical operations as well as logistics. Central to its thinking, therefore, was the idea of the helicopter gunship that could fire high explosive rockets and grenades as well as direct-fire machine guns. If Aerial Rocket Artillery could replace conventional artillery, it was reasoned, then absolutely all the functions of a conventional overland assault could be performed by helicopters using the revolutionary technique of "vertical envelopment." In stark contrast to the constraints affecting earlier operations, the attacking force could skip blithely over all obstacles at speeds in excess of 100 mph, thereby achieving surprise, shock and a massive economy of force.

The eventual result of General Hamilton H. Howze's deliberations would be the 1st Cavalry (Airmobile) Division, activated on 1st July 1965. Before that moment arrived, however, intensive combat experience with helicopters was already being gained by US military advisers – and some full Army Helicopter Companies – in support of the Army of the Republic of South Vietnam (ARVN). From 1959 and during all the Kennedy years the security situation in Indochina had been deteriorating under a widespread Viet Cong assault supported and directed by North Vietnam. President Ngo Dinh Diem had been unable to find a solution and, when he was toppled and killed, just three weeks before Kennedy's own assassination, the situation grew no better. The USA was rapidly being presented with a stark choice between cutting her losses and leaving South Vietnam to the impending communist takeover, or making a major military intervention that would reverse the situation and keep Vietnam free.

In August 1964 the Gulf of Tonkin incident provoked President Lyndon B. Johnson into gradually moving towards the second alternative. America's international prestige was riding higher

*Santo Domingo demonstrators jeer members of the US 82nd Airborne Division – apparently good-humoredly – in September 1965. Agitation would continue until the political crisis was resolved by orderly elections held in June the following year.*

than ever in these years, and she was now better armed and more ready to take on the fight than she had been at any time since 1945. Besides, she had already supported the abstract ideal of a South Vietnam for too long to be willing to quit now. Johnson therefore started taking direct military action: first with Operation "Pierce Arrow," "Flaming Dart" and "Rolling Thunder" air strikes against North Vietnam; then on 8th March 1965 with the landing of two Marine battalions at Da Nang. The build up of ground forces would continue through 1967, with increasingly large scale and more aggressive "Search and Destroy" combat actions being fought.

In August 1965 Operation "Starlite" was a regimental sweep by the marines southeast of Da Nang against some 1,500 VC who initially stood firm to fight it out, but suffered crippling casualties and then exfiltrated out of contact overnight. This was to become an all too familiar pattern in many battles that were yet to come. In October-November the battle of the Ia Drang Valley involved most of the newly-arrived 1st Cavalry (Airmobile) Division against the equivalent of a North Vietnamese Army (NVA) division. At first responding to calls for help by beleaguered freeworld garrisons, the 1st Cavalry moved swiftly to convert its operation into a violent pursuit against a withdrawing enemy. In the process a battalion sized US force was temporarily pinned down at Landing Zone "X Ray" with some 270 casualties, of whom over half were killed – a shocking total for an army that had become accustomed to an average of only 25 killed in action per year in Vietnam between 1961 and 1963. Nevertheless, the enemy was eventually hounded all the way back to his Cambodian sanctuaries with the loss of some 3,000 casualties as against 830 US.

Operation "Masher/White Wing" was also big, mounted by the 1st Cavalry Division between January and March 1966 in Binh Dinh province, although it failed to catch as many enemy as in the Ia Drang. Further south the 25th Infantry Division was discovering the fearsome Cu Chi tunnels west of Saigon, while a few months later the 1st ("Big Red One") Infantry Division's operations in the notoriously heavily fortified "Iron Triangle" and War Zone "C," just north of Saigon, set new records for stiff fighting in this war. The culmination came in Operation "Attleboro" between September and November, when some 22,000 men were involved, of whom about 650 were casualties for an estimated enemy loss of at least 1,100 dead. Between January and May 1967 Operations "Cedar Falls" and "Junction City" would be mounted at Corps level in very much the same areas – against an enemy Corps that would suffer an estimated 3,550 killed in action

for around 354 US dead. Apparently, however, the overall strategic effect was somewhat spoiled when McNamara came to read J. Schell's book entitled *The Village of Ben Suc*. This graphically showed the Secretary of Defense just how unreal was his impersonally "managerial" language of cost-benefit analysis, body counts and hamlet evaluations, when set beside the harsh human realities of the shooting war. In Operation "Cedar Falls" Ben Suc's inhabitants had been abused and relocated, then their homes razed, for no very clear purpose beyond a somewhat rarefied refugee-creation policy intended to make it easier to establish free fire zones. A sense of the futility of the whole approach began to seep into the higher levels of government, and McNamara

RIGHT

*A pre-packaged Christmas dinner is hastily enjoyed by a patrol of 82nd Airborne in the Santo Domingo dock area, 1965. Note the novel infantry weaponry that seemed revolutionary at the time – the M60 machine gun for hammer-drill direct fire, and the M79 "blooper" grenade launcher for close support indirect fire.*

BELOW

*Secretary of Defense Robert S. McNamara (right), chief architect of the radical new US strategy created in the early 1960s. Here he talks with Senator John Stennis, chairman of the Senate Armed Forces Preparedness Investigating Sub-committee on the air war in North Vietnam, August 1967.*

would resign in November 1967 over disagreements with the President on the bombing policy.

Quite apart from the humanitarian doubts that were spreading fast among the nation's students and journalists by 1967, the whole package of US strategy in Indochina was also becoming painfully frustrating to the military themselves. The first point was that no amount of bombing in Operation "Rolling Thunder" against North Vietnam, or in Operation "Igloo White" against the Ho Chi Minh trail through Laos and Cambodia, seemed to be sufficient to persuade the NVA to stop sending troops and war stores into South Vietnam. Secondly, diplomatic considerations prevented these bombing campaigns from being reinforced by ground forces going into the "sanctuaries." Laos, Cambodia and North Vietnam therefore remained as safe havens, secure from hot pursuit, just as China north of the Yalu had been during the Korean War. Whenever the communists felt they were being too roughly handled by the Americans inside South Vietnam, they could simply flit away over the border to rest, regroup and reequip.

This in turn led to an impossibly demanding defensive strategy within the south. General William C. Westmoreland, US commander in Vietnam, was not permitted to make strategic counter-strokes into neighboring countries; yet he was expected to prevent all small unit – or even individual – NVA infiltrations across an inaccessible jungle frontier some 800 miles long. He never had force numbers that were anything like adequate to stake out the whole of this line – and in fact his available "teeth arms" were very

often outnumbered by the in-country NVA. As a final humiliation, this imbalance implied that US forces in South Vietnam had to conduct a mobile but indecisive and attritional defense, lunging first to one threatened section of the frontier, and then to another. As soon as each operation had been concluded, all the ground won would in effect be handed straight back to the enemy. Only the kill ratio could be claimed as an indicator of victory in such operations; but precisely because the enemy could always escape to his sanctuaries to regroup, he could never be made to suffer a level of losses that he would find genuinely unacceptable. To use Joseph Heller's mythological WWII Air Force phrase, the whole logic of US strategy in Vietnam was thus condemned from the first to be a "Catch 22 Situation." It was the NVA's cross-border sanctuaries that forced the Army to win just by attrition; but the cutting edge of attrition was itself severely blunted precisely by the existence of the cross-border sanctuaries.

Attrition also cut two ways, because it was not just the enemy's dead that could have a political impact on the outcome of the war: it was also Uncle Sam's. When American troops first went into Vietnam they were expecting to face a relatively low level of opposition, and hence a relatively low level of casualties. What they found, however, was that North Vietnam responded to the US deployment by a greatly intensified deployment of her own. Instead of a scattering of VC guerrillas, the Americans soon found themselves facing formed battalions, regiments and divisions of regular NVA jungle fighters. The battles grew quickly in scale – and US casualties rose accordingly. Even though there might be a kill ratio of ten to one in favor of the Americans (and by 1972 it would be no less than 34 to one), the absolute number of US casualties still showed a severe increase. In a war that was perceived at home as important and "conventional," such as the two World Wars or Korea, this would have been accepted. In Vietnam, however, there was a general bafflement and frustration that the war was so unseizable, so undeclared and so unconventional; that the generals kept promising victory, but no victory seemed to come. The pain of bereavement was very real, but the cause for which it was imposed seemed remote and unreal.

LEFT

*President John F. Kennedy briefs the press on the growing communist menace to Laos, March 1961. US interest in the defence of Indochina had already been strong before the French defeat of 1954, but the confident Kennedy years marked a dramatic upturn in commitment. By 1965 there would be some 20,000 US advisers in-country.*

By 1968 the general frustration with these apparently purposeless casualties would become a major political motor behind the anti-war movement.

Another cause of unrest was the selective draft itself, which in a major declared war like Korea would have been mitigated by a call out of the widely-based Army Reserve. For Vietnam, however, the President refused to abandon the fiction that it was "business as usual," and would not employ the Reserve in combat. This allowed the burden of combat to fall disproportionately upon unexempted or undeferred draftees, usually drawn from the least advantaged sections of society. Not only did they themselves increasingly come to resent this perceived unfairness in the system, but their lot added potent fuel to resistance to the draft. To add injury to insult, the failure to activate the Reserve also exacerbated a shortage of many types of highly trained technicians within the warzone – particularly helicopter pilots, whose esoteric skills were so vital to every operation.

A still deeper strategic difficulty was that there were really two wars being fought simultaneously within South Vietnam, but the USA was fighting only one of them. This was the "mainforce" war against large units of heavily-armed enemy, usually NVA coming in from the outside. Westmoreland saw his role as putting up a shield in the lightly-populated border areas, to keep these intruders away from the mass of the South Vietnamese population living in the villages along the coast. The Americans were therefore "holding the ring" while their ARVN allies went ahead with the job of suppressing VC guerrilla activity in the "village" war. However, the fallacy inherent in this approach was the assumption that the ARVN was competent to win the village war on its own. It was precisely because it had been nearly overwhelmed in this role by 1965 that US troops had been committed in the first place – and in 1966 the ARVN was still suffering from many cases of combat refusal. Besides, the ARVN had not originally been built up by the Americans to fight a counter-insurgency war at all, but rather for conventional war on the ROK pattern. When it came to fighting the VC in the villages, it found itself inappropriately trained and equipped, and badly hamstrung by governmental corruption. Until the VC chose to commit Hari-Kiri in the 1968 Tet offensive, therefore, the ARVN had been unable to make any real headway against it.

During this time US numbers in-country were nevertheless steadily rising towards a 1968 peak of some 600,000 men, despite considerable logistic difficulties in creating port, airfield and base facilities. Familiar tactics and weaponry were also gradually being adapted in novel ways to cope with what seemed to be a very different style of conflict from either the Korean model of "limited

*US military adviser Captain Linton Beasley (right) overseeing weapon training in a squad of the Army of the Republic of Vietnam (ARVN), 1962. The M1 carbine and Al Capone-vintage Thompson gun were useful automatics for the small-statured Vietnamese; but it was to be an unduly long time before the superior M16 Armalite would be released to America's allies.*

*An ARVN 21st Division bugler signals a mortar team across open ground during an attack on Viet Cong (VC) positions in the Mekong Delta in 1967. Controlling the approaches to Saigon, the low lying Delta region would long be an important battlefield for free world forces.*

*Lieutenant Don Burchell of the US Big Red One Division sends a shiver of protest around the world by implementing a "scorched earth" policy at Lai Khe. Actually the military aim of this strategic hamlet program was to destroy outlying dwellings occupied by Viet Cong sympathizers, thereby concentrating villagers in a central location that could be policed.*

**VIETNAM**

war," or the Guadalcanal model of "jungle war." For example, a specialized USN riverine force was created for the Mekong Delta – a "brown water navy" that came complete with armored landing craft, command boats, medevac boats, monitors, artillery barges and even a brigade-sized floating base. Also in the Delta, General Julian J. Ewell's 9th Division made sustained tactical experiments with light infantry and helicopter-borne commando techniques, including a specialized sniper program and the famed "people sniffer" – an ammonia-monitoring proboscis dangled from a helicopter.

Above all, the unconventional nature of the terrain and tactics in Vietnam made this war a natural candidate for the first massive use of helicopters and the new airmobile concepts. This was not just a matter of the experimental airmobile division, but spilled out into all other formations as well. By the end of 1967 every US infantry division was effectively airmobile in all but name, since it could call upon helicopter lift for several of its battalions at any one time. Some 4,000 rotary wing machines were available in-country, as compared to the paltry 42 that had been deployed by the French in 1954. In fact, American officers who had studied the vicissitudes of the First Indochina War had determined not to repeat the French "mistake" of relying on ground-based transportation that could apparently be ambushed so easily. With the arrival of the helicopter they seemed to sense that conventional trucks, armor and artillery were now almost entirely obsolete. An especially low priority was put on the deployment of armored vehicles – tanks and Armored Cavalry Assault Vehicles (ACAVs) – even though these had quickly been found to possess the protection, impetus and direct fire capability that was required to help an infantry assault forward through an enemy bunker position.

Until about 1967 it was widely believed that the tank's role could be adequately performed by armed helicopters, especially the purpose-built Huey Cobra gunship (or "Snake") that would soon be coming into service. What was missed, however, was that although such weapons had many essential uses in armed reconnaissance, escorting transport helicopters and developing prep. fires, they could not roll forward in front of the infantry providing an armored screen. Once the troops had moved away from an LZ and its attendant helicopters, they would be no better armed than the enemy, and would feel personally vulnerable and exposed. Nor was the gunship's main armament, the 2.75" rocket salvo, always effective against dug-in targets in the jungle. Something heavier with a higher velocity was needed, in the shape of a tank gun. Thus by 1968 there was a certain reversion to earlier tactics, with the helicopter being placed in a more realistic relationship to the other arms than some of its more absolutist champions might have wished. Like every new weapon, it had to take its place as part of an all-arms team: it could not win the war on its own.

Something similar must be said of another major innovation in military technology that was coming forward fast in 1967-8. This was the idea of the "electronic battlefield," whereby a wide area of terrain could be wired up with automatic sensors to detect any enemy movement through it. When signals were received that a target was present, conventional air and artillery strikes could be called down to obliterate it. Clearly this offered a highly futuristic vision of remote-controlled warfare that side-stepped the need for infantry on the ground altogether. It seemed to be an ideal "combat multiplier" that precisely suited the American need to minimize casualties in limited wars.

The electronic battlefield was first used along the Ho Chi Minh trail, supported by airpower working out of Thailand as part of Operation "Igloo White." A total of some 35,000 enemy trucks would eventually be claimed destroyed in this program during the war. Within South Vietnam a big deployment of electronic sensors to prevent infiltration was also due to be made in 1968 along the inappropriately-name "Demilitarized Zone," that ran along the frontier with North Vietnam. This was to become the "McNamara Line," although in the event its electronic equipment was diverted to help in the defense of the Khe Sanh combat base during the Tet Offensive. Its performance there was patchy, and many technical problems were encountered. Nevertheless, the sensors did play a useful part in the concerted fire program that would eventually turn Khe Sanh into a major killing field for the NVA. By 1969 the technology would be improved, and used to excellent effect in battles such as FSB Crook, and in the 11th Cavalry Regiment's 1970 trap-lines in III Corps area.

By the end of 1967 the USA had completed the deployment of very major forces to South Vietnam, although they were still inadequate to mount a solid territorial defense all along the border. They

ABOVE

*US Marines wading through rice paddies at Hoa My near Da Nang air base, soon after their first arrival in South Vietnam, 1965. This patrol encountered a VC ambush a few moments after the photograph was taken, losing four casualties and inflicting five.*

ABOVE

*Another marine patrol scours the ricelands around Da Nang, 1965.*

LEFT

*Marines intercept VC messages during an ambush south of Da Nang, September 1966. Lieutenant Colonel Victor Ohanesian listens in while the enemy speaks in Chinese, ready to pass the receiver to ARVN Lieutenant Droung Due Dhuy when the broadcast switches to Vietnamese.*

had been hammered by escalating NVA attacks, but were perfecting their weapons and tactics and were starting to win the upper hand. By 1970 the enemy would be containable within relatively restricted border enclaves. However, there were still big holes in US strategy for the village war and for hot pursuit into the enemy's sanctuaries. The hope of victory was based too much on attrition, which made the general US posture weaker than it need have been. This was to be made cruelly obvious at the start of 1968, when the VC launched its New Year Tet offensive.

ABOVE

*Marines on patrol in heavy bush near Da Nang. In jungle warfare the tactical problem was often that only a "one man front" could be employed, making it difficult to deploy a wide base of fire against ambushes.*

RIGHT

*A much-photographed Vietnamese ox cart overshadowed by a column of M48 tanks of the 173rd Airborne Division, symbolizing the clash of cultures in the battle for Saigon, 1966.*

RIGHT

*A Marine cradles his 7.62 mm M14 automatic rifle while his buddy calls up an air strike against engaged elements of an estimated North Vietnamese division. Operation Hastings, Dong Ha 1966.*

*Patrolling the rice paddies north of Saigon in the 82nd Airborne Division's shallow-draft air boats, September 1969. This is one example of a whole range of imaginative new technologies that were brought forth by the war. Others included hovercraft, silent airplanes and "people sniffing" helicopters.*

*Dead North Vietnamese infiltrators on Highway 15 at Ben Cat, 25 miles from Saigon.*

RIGHT

*Fifty-five demonstrators were arrested in the anti-war march in Chicago's Grant Park on 26th August 1968, at the time of the Democratic National Convention. The protest would escalate during the next two days and nights.*

BELOW

*National Guardsmen armed with Garand rifles, machine guns and tear gas prepare to give their all in defence of central Chicago, 28th August 1968. In the event thousands of anti-war protestors succeeded in breaking through police and National Guard lines.*

*An F-4 Phantom jet "Bombing trees" in the jungle war. Forward air controllers, circling in light slow aircraft, would keep close contact with troops on the ground. When they had identified and marked targets for the "fast movers," heavy ordnance loads of explosive or napalm could be dropped with considerable accuracy.*

*B-52 bombers fly an "Arclight" bombing raid over the seriously mis-named "Demilitarized Zone" between the two Vietnams, October 1967. In this particular operation a total of 1.5 million pounds of bombs were dropped on North Vietnamese artillery positions in the course of three days.*

*Two ageing Navy Skyhawks take their bombloads to North Vietnam in 1967 during Operation Rolling Thunder – the failed attempt to blitz the invader to the conference table by carefully graduated bombing interspersed by pauses to receive diplomatic signals. By the 1968 presidential election it would be the USA that had, in effect, bombed itself into withdrawal from the war.*

# CHAPTER EIGHT

# THE NAM (2)

*From Tet to Mayaguez, 1968-75*

Throughout years of war the South Vietnamese government had often been forced to abandon the villages and the countryside to VC control; but it had always been secure in the cities and provincial capitals. The war was generally fought out of town, over issues that concerned the ownership of farming land even more than higher questions of national reunification or resistance to foreign interference. By 1968, however, the VC had determined to change all this by bringing the war unexpectedly and violently into the town centers themselves. Some 84,000 VC and NVA soldiers would infiltrate quietly during the days before the Tet (lunar New Year) national holiday, to launch a surprise attack on that day, 31st January. They would be helped by the customary ceasefire and ARVN leave period during the holiday – and also by diversionary operations to pin down the Americans in the remote border regions, notably at Khe Sanh.

*Fierce house-to-house fighting for Hue, 3rd February.*

*Marines clearing the ancient Vietnamese capital city of Hue three days after it had been overrun by the Viet Cong in their shock 31st January 1968 Tet Offensive. Here a machine gun team overwatches an infantry squad cautiously checking out a suburban villa.*

In the event surprise was very nearly complete, despite a number of what should have been giveaway early attacks on 30th January. In Saigon several exceptionally daring raids were made, not least against the US embassy itself. This event deeply disillusioned the US public, who asked how such such a thing could still be possible after over three years of high intensity warfare and sacrifice. Their sense of unease was only too quickly reinforced by film of the summary execution of a VC suspect by the Saigon police chief, and by a US Army officer explaining how he had to "destroy this town in order to save it." To television viewers back home it seemed that the war had run completely out of control and, despite bland official assurances to the contrary, victory was visibly receding.

Actually the military facts were diametrically opposite to the popular perception, since although Tet did produce the highest daily rate of US casualties so far in the war, it also produced incomparably the highest VC loss rate. In every town where armed communists appeared, they were repulsed or shot down, usually within a matter of hours rather than days. They are thought to have suffered a staggering total of some 40,000 dead. This was enough to tear the guts out of the VC as a country-wide political and guerrilla movement, and it would never thereafter have a significant role to play.

The longest and hardest battles of the Tet offensive were fought in the center of Hue, the ancient imperial capital, and in the siege of the Khe Sanh combat base on the extreme northwest border. Ironically it was the NVA's feint attack against the latter that actually involved them in their greatest Tet casualties of all – over 10,000 dead as against around 5,000 in Hue. Perhaps this imbalance was due mainly to President Johnson's personal determination that Khe Sanh should not become a new Dien Bien Phu – the fortified base whose fall in 1954 had decided French defeat in the First Indochina War. The historical parallels between the two sieges were certainly arresting, since both were prosecuted by the same man – General Vo Nguyen Giap – and both were desperate defences of low-lying landing strips dominated by a circle of hills.

Two NVA divisions had seized some – but not all – of the key positions around Khe Sanh by the time of the Tet offensive, and they would tighten their grip during the following two weeks. On 7th February they overran an outlying firebase at Lang Vei with PT 76 light tanks – an innovation that represented an ominous escalation in their weaponry. They also maintained a terrific bombardment of the main base, limiting the use of the runway just to small aircraft and helicopters that had to take off almost as soon as they landed. Despite the poor – monsoon – flying conditions,

an ambitious resupply operation was nevertheless mounted for the 6,700 marines of the garrison (mainly from the 26th Marine Regiment), and it was ultimately very successful.

Still more awesome was the deployment of firepower to suppress the assailants. Techniques for making rapid combinations of artillery and air strikes were developed, and given appropriate names such as "Killer Junior," "Killer Senior" and "Mini Arclight." The aircraft employed went from humble and ageing – but essential – O1E Bird Dog Forward Air Control light spotter planes, all the way up to B52 Stratofortresses flying "Arclight" carpet bombing missions in sticks of three aircraft, each stick dropping some 160,000 pounds of bombs within a few seconds. Free from the restrictions of civilian towns in the neighborhood, the whole area around Khe Sanh became a lethal free fire zone for the 77 days of the siege. The attack withered away until, between 1st and 8th April, the base was relieved in Operation "Pegasus" – a large scale airmobile sweep by 1st

Cavalry Division. About 1,050 US casualties had been incurred during the siege, which became a symbol of the marines' determination and fighting qualities. However, mobile strategy and manpower overstretch meant that the base itself would have to be evacuated and demolished before the fall.

Yet another gruelling test for the marines had been in Hue, where most of the city had been quickly overrun by the enemy at the start of the Tet offensive, with the brutal murder of some 5,000 civilians. The 1st & 5th Marine Regiments had the task of counter attacking and clearing the tightly-packed buildings of the "New City" suburb to the south of the Perfume river. This proved to be a very tough mission indeed, and the troops had to learn new skills of house-to-house fighting. On 11th February the marines' responsibility was further extended when ARVN airborne forces called for help in retaking the ancient walled citadel – which included another maze of easily-defended buildings. Final success was achieved

*Wounded marines litter the street in Hue on 5th February as the realization begins to sink in that this will be a long, hard battle after all. Air power, armor and artillery proved unable to cut quickly through the determined defenses.*

LEFT

*A Marine M48 tank advances through the war-torn streets of Hue covered by a tracked 6-barrelled Ontos tank destroyer, 3rd February 1968. The recapture of the city would be prematurely announced three days later; but to widespread stateside disappointment it was not finally achieved until the 24th.*

only on 24th February, at the cost of almost 1,000 US and 400 ARVN casualties.

After Tet there were continuing freeworld follow-up operations and "accelerated pacification" programs throughout the rest of 1968, as well as a generally suicidal communist "Mini-Tet" offensive in May through August. These actions would all help cement the defeat of the enemy in the village war, and push the NVA mainforce units back to the largely uninhabited border regions. In the meantime, however, the presidential campaign being fought in the USA would provide a focus for the widespread anti-war feeling that Tet had brought to the surface. As the chief architect of direct US intervention in Vietnam, President Johnson announced at the end of March that he would not run for reelection. It was found that all the leading candidates from both parties were in favor of ending the war, either sooner or later, in the course of their four year term. In the event the election of President Richard M. Nixon represented one of the more conservative among the options available, since he wanted a relatively slow wind down in the US commitment – and would show himself quite capable of expanding the war in order to end it. Nevertheless, this should not obscure the fact that his ultimate aim was still to obtain disengagement – which he and his National Security Adviser Henry Kissinger skillfully achieved by the start of 1973.

Nixon's policy was to boost the already-existing concept of "Vietnamization." Whereas Johnson, McNamara and Westmoreland had shouldered the ARVN aside to give the maximum combat role to US forces, the new Republican government wished to reverse that trend. The ARVN would be upgraded to the point where it could fight the mainforce war as well as the village war on its own, allowing American ground troops to pull out, except for a few specialists. The US contribution to South Vietnam's security would eventually consist only of logistic, air, naval and financial support. Given the improving situation on the ground in the aftermath of Tet, this was by no means an unrealistic policy, and it would be helped still further by a willingness to break old rules by entering the enemy's sanctuaries in Laos and Cambodia, and even by bombing downtown Hanoi. Nixon and Kissinger believed in negotiating from a dynamic – not to mention worryingly unpredictable – posture, and it paid dividends.

General Creighton W. Abrams succeeded

LEFT

*On 16th February medics rush to the rescue of a wounded Marine in the escalating fight for the Hue citadel, an imposing seventeenth century fortress that proved to be a very expensive nut to crack.*

Westmoreland in the Vietnam command in June 1968, and started laying the foundations for the Vietnamization program almost at once. The level of US commitment to combat started to decline, with one of the last "old style" slugging matches coming at "Hamburger Hill" in the A Shau valley in May 1969. This action gained particular notoriety when it was condemned by Senator Edward Kennedy as "senseless and irresponsible," not least because the ground won was soon relinquished to the enemy. However, in ten days' hard fighting the Americans suffered just 70 killed in action, which actually compares very favorably not just with the 630 NVA bodies counted, but with the 304 US dead in the Ia Drang battle of 1965, not to mention the far more than 1,000 at Belleau Wood in 1918 – or the 99 percent wiped out at the Alamo in 1836. In almost any other circumstances Hamburger Hill could have been represented as a glorious success – but in the sour public mood of 1969 it was written down as a major humiliation and defeat.

The public's opposition to the war eventually reached the soldiers themselves, once it had become clear that the US commitment was winding down. Whereas they had previously been ready to fight and die for victory, nobody any longer wanted even to be wounded in the lack-lustre cause of "phased withdrawal." Just one casualty in any unit started to look like a casualty too many, and army cohesion visibly sagged. Some units were tempted into committing atrocities as a means of venting their frustration, in deliberate breach of the very tight official rules of engagement. Indiscipline, slackness, combat refusal, racial agitation and drugs took a heavy toll, where previously there had been a taut, highly-tuned fighting machine. The American ground forces tended to retire to their base areas and stay there, while the government in Washington resignedly began to think about dismantling the inequitable draft and redesigning strategy around a "one and a half war" standard in the place of McNamara's two and a half.

The rescue of friendly casualties also came to the fore as a major issue within the US forces. Whereas in past wars it had always been seen as proper and decent to look after wounded comrades if there was a chance to do so, this now became a matter of overriding importance – "more sacred than life itself," as one officer expressed it. Whole battle plans would therefore be distorted to rescue an individual airman who had ejected; or assaults would be suspended to arrange for the casevac of the injured – and sometimes even of the dead. Contrary to normal practice, the rule in Vietnam was that those killed in action were returned to their homes in the USA, not buried where they fell. In a limited war it seemed as though deaths were somehow less acceptable

than usual, and military operations against the enemy were given secondary priority to the solemn processes of mourning.

In the same general area, a particularly intractable problem was the recovery of prisoners captured by the enemy. This had already been a major issue during the Korean War, but it became still more prominent in the 1970s. On 21 November 1970 US special forces had mounted a complex night helicopter incursion deep into North Vietnam to rescue the inmates of Son Tay prison camp, only to find it contained no Americans. Photographic reconnaissance by Remotely Piloted Vehicles (RPVs) had proved defective, since it was a new technology that had not yet been perfected. There was a firefight with some "East Europeans," but no rescue. Eventually the Americans held in North Vietnam had to be extracted by diplomatic negotiation, as part

---

RIGHT

*Apart from the bitter battle for Hue, the 1968 Tet Offensive involved especially heavy combat in the siege of the Marine Corps' Khe Sanh Combat Base, where just two lines of infantry trenches protected the densely-packed central mass of berms, bunkers and dumps. Note the foreground, where wriggling trenches and bomb craters are reminscent of the Western Front in WWI.*

---

BELOW

*A CH-46 Sea Knight airlifts supplies to Marines in the "boonies." The helicopter brought vast new mobility to the battlefields of Vietnam, where ground movement was often very difficult indeed.*

*Marine Corps tank crews at Khe Sanh observe air strikes around the perimeter of their overlooked stronghold. President Lyndon B. Johnson took a particular personal interest in the fate of the garrison, and pulled out all the stops to support it.*

of the 1973 peace agreement. In Operation "Homecoming" some 591 were ferried back to the States; but there was widespread suspicion that others had not been declared by Hanoi. Some 1,903 missing servicemen and civilians remained unaccounted for, and it is conceivable that a few are still held to this day. In the prevailing wartime conditions of psychic barbarity and jungle terrain, however, it is highly likely that most died.

For all the American problems during the last few years of their involvement, Vietnamization went ahead successfully and soon started to show results. In May and June 1970 a major assault on communist sanctuaries in Cambodia was a particular success, despite the enemy's avoidance of battle. Unexpectedly vast stockpiles of equipment were discovered in the "Parrot's Beak" and "Fish Hook" areas north of Saigon, and it became clear that a big enemy offensive had been pre-empted. Many American soldiers wryly reflected on the advantages that might have been gained by such "hot pursuit" actions if they had been taken earlier in the war. Only the dubious legality of the operation spoiled the military achievement, since it led to an uproar of protest at

home and the killing of four Kent State students by the National Guard on 4th May. This in turn helped accelerate the pace of US withdrawal.

A new incursion was planned against the Ho Chi Minh trail for February of the following year, this time through Tchepone in Laos. US armor and artillery would clear the road as far as the border in Operation "Dewey Canyon II", then the ARVN would make the final assault on their own, as Operation "Lam Son 719." On this occasion, however, the enemy's resistance proved overwhelming. Ambushing every road and every LZ, then mounting effective assaults against improvised ARVN firebases, including attacks with tanks, the NVA soon created a panic rout. The South Vietnamese troops streamed back across the border, having suffered some 7,000 casualties in a month of combat. US losses over the same period had been 1,350, but claims were filed that the NVA had lost 20,000.

Lam Son 719 was a setback for Vietnamization, but a still harder blow was now being prepared. In almost a mirror image of the US transfer of modern arms to South Vietnam, the USSR was now sending large supplies of modern tanks, artillery and SAMs to the north. A three pronged Easter offensive was being organized for 1972 that would take advantage of the American presidential elections and the supposed shakiness of the ARVN. Starting across the DMZ on 30th March, it at first swept all before it, and began to drive the ARVN 3rd Division back through Quang Tri. Then a second assault aimed at Saigon began on 5th April and soon approached An Loc.

It was at this point, however, that South

Vietnamese resistance firmed up and they held the line, both at An Loc and in a new line south of Quang Tri. President Nixon ordered a major movement of air power across the Pacific to support them, and resumed bombing the north in Operation "Linebacker I." This broke a number of established conventions for the air war, since it included B52s flying strategic, not tactical, missions. It also included the use of "smart" bombs for the economical destruction of bridges, the mining of Haiphong Harbor, and an intensified interdiction program along the routes leading south. Now that the NVA had turned to conventional warfare, it offered more conventional – and therefore more vulnerable – targets to freeworld airmen. For example, within South Vietnam helicopters proved their effectiveness against tanks, especially when they used the new TOW guided missile.

General Giap launched a new attack in the Central Highlands at the end of April, but Kontum was stoutly defended by ARVN troops under the guidance of John Paul Vann, a famous Indochina hand. The NVA was therefore stalled all along the line, and was quickly running out of reserves. By June their forces were pinned down conducting a series of sieges, while airpower – supplemented by naval gunfire along the coast – continued to batter them. They were forced to withdraw in September, leaving behind some 100,000 casualties and a much more self-confident ARVN than had been seen in earlier years.

The ARVN's ability to fight nevertheless remained heavily dependent on US support, both financial and in the form of air strikes. This was assured during the remainder of 1972, while peace terms were being negotiated between the USA, the two Vietnams and the VC. When the talks stalled in December, Nixon ordered a resumption

ABOVE RIGHT

*Marine 175 mm self-propelled long-range artillery in the Rock Pile Firebase, supporting the Khe Sanh garrison from a range of twelve miles. During the Operation Pegasus relief of Khe Sanh by 1st Cavalry Division (Airmobile) in April, this would be the initial assembly point.*

RIGHT

*Once the decision to withdraw from Vietnam had been taken in the backwash of the Tet Offensive, politicians felt more free to criticize the handling of the fighting. Senator Edward Kennedy made an especially pointed critique of the gruelling May 1969 assault on Hamburger Hill in the A Shau Valley. Newly-elected President Nixon, by contrast, decided it was time to fight all the harder to cover the pull-out.*

of bombing in Operation "Linebacker II" – an intense period of thirteen days in which Hanoi and Haiphong were flattened without any of the restrictions that had earlier so frustrated the aircrews. Losses of US aircraft reached 26, but the enemy was brought back to the conference table and graciously agreed to allow the Americans to withdraw from Indochina. It was scarcely a concession, however, since the completion of US disengagement in March 1973 became the signal for Congress to cut back dramatically on aid to the South. The line of reasoning seemed to be "If the war is over, why should US dollars and aircraft still be used to fight it?" There were, of course, other strands to the argument, not least of which were the Watergate scandal and the belief that the President was taking too many war powers to himself. Nor did anyone want a situation in which US ground troops might one day be drawn back into Vietnam. To prevent any possibility of this happening, Congress effectively cut off all its residual commitments to the war.

This left the South Vietnamese without any visible means of support. They had counted on Nixon's promise that the USA would never let them down; but now they found that this was precisely what was happening. The flow of cash, ammunition and fuel to sustain the ARVN dried up, and morale evaporated. When the next communist offensive was launched in January 1975 it scored some initial local successes that provoked a disastrous re-positioning of South Vietnamese forces. During the move out of the Central Highlands the roads became blocked and the ARVN troops were caught on the line of march by the NVA. Resistance then collapsed apart from a few heroic last stands, as at Xuan Loc. Saigon fell on 30th April amid scenes of panic in the evacuation.

The US had mounted Operation "Frequent Wind" to pull out their nationals and Vietnamese officials compromised with the incoming regime; but it could not cope with the vast numbers of Vietnamese who wanted to escape. Nor was there room on the aircraft carriers for all the helicopters

*Here a stretcher party of 101st Airborne Division rushes to save a comrade hit by enemy fire from Hamburger Hill.*

*Wounded ARVN paratroops retiring from fierce combat to break the North Vietnamese encirclement of Ben Het Special Forces camp, June 1969. As Vietnamization of the war went ahead, the ARVN became successively more responsible for their own defense.*

that came out, some of which had to be pushed into the sea. As the closing act of the greatest helicopter war in history, however, this memorable image was surely only too bitterly appropriate.

Actually it was not *quite* the last act of the war, since on 12th May 1975 there was one further incident that also, in its way, encapsulated both the valor and the frustrations of the whole Indochina war. This came when Cambodian Khmer Rouge gunboats seized the US Liberty ship *Mayaguez* in international waters. The ship itself was soon recaptured, but the crew of 39 was believed to have been taken hostage to nearby Koh Tang island. President Gerald Ford therefore dispatched a strong helicopter-borne force of marines to rescue them on 15th May. Unfortunately, however, this came into a "hot LZ" and was brought under intense fire as it tried to land on the beach. Several HH-53 "Jolly Green" helicopters were destroyed almost immediately, and by the end of the operation only two out of fifteen would remain unscathed. The operation quickly escalated until there was half a battalion of marines in contact with the enemy, even though they failed to find the hostages. A 15,000lb "Daisy Cutter" blast bomb had to be used to create a new LZ to extract the force overnight. Meanwhile the *Mayaguez'* crew had already been independently released, so the assault landing with its 68 US casualties – including 18 killed in action – may have been unnecessary after all.

TOP

*A student protest against President Nixon's war policy in New York, October 1969.*

ABOVE LEFT

*Ohio National Guards "advance to contact" against Cambodia demonstrators in Kent State University, 4th May 1970. Their fire would kill four students and badly exacerbate the souring of the domestic political atmosphere.*

ABOVE

*Pro-war construction workers assail Cambodia
demonstrators in Wall Street as police stand back,
8th May 1970. New York's Mayor John V. Lindsay
condemned this over-robust defense of the American
right to invade neutral countries.*

**ABOVE**

*The first strike authorized into North Vietnamese sanctuaries came in Nixon's controversial incursion into Cambodia in the spring of 1970. Here allied officers inspect large quantities of North Vietnamese medical supplies captured in the "Fishhook" area on 3rd May.*

**LEFT**

*Perhaps the most reassuring sight in Vietnam jungle warfare was the Medevac Huey Dustoff helicopter. Here a South Vietnamese Ranger is landed to be rushed to hospital through the Khe Sanh Combat Base, after being wounded in one of the catastrophic firefights in Operation Lamson 719, eastern Laos early 1971.*

ABOVE

*A young ARVN soldier raises his grenade launcher against North Vietnamese raiders some fourteen miles outside Saigon on 31st October 1972. He was cut down moments later, to die in the arms of the photographer.*

RIGHT

*Mass imports of mothballed US equipment for the ARVN forces arrive in Da Nang during November 1972, in a last-minute attempt to bolster Vietnamization ahead of the negotiated cease-fire deadline. This was the "defensive" part of the US plan: the lethal "offensive" side would hit Hanoi a few days later in the form of intense bombing during Operation Linebacker 2.*

ABOVE

*President Nixon explaining policy to Secretary of State Henry Kissinger on board Air Force One, en route to NATO talks and the Moscow summit in Europe, July 1974. The two men had conducted impressive "shuttle diplomacy" with the communist world throughout the crucial previous years; but their partnership would soon be blown apart by the Watergate impeachment.*

*Operation Frequent Wind: the searingly memorable scene as an Air America Huey helicopter evacuates Americans and others fleeing from downtown Saigon as North Vietnamese spearheads thrust rapidly to occupy what would soon be re-named Ho Chi Minh City, 29th April 1975.*

*Secretary of State Kissinger discusses the postwar world with President Gerald Ford in the White House Oval Office, October 1975. In May of that year President Ford had ordered the ill-starred rescue of the hi-jacked liberty ship* Mayaguez.

# CHAPTER NINE

# WALKING TALL

*Operations since 1975*

While the Vietnam war was still in progress, America clearly demonstrated the extent of both her military power and her willingness to make heavy sacrifices in support of allies threatened by communist aggression. All this sent powerful deterrent signals to Moscow for a period of more than ten years, reinforcing an impression of Western determination and strength that had already been conveyed during the Cuban Missile Crisis. However, the Vietnam war also revealed a collapse of national – and NATO – unity that was to have immensely damaging consequences in the aftermath of the 1973 peace treaty. Not only was South Vietnam itself then left to its fate, but an impression was conveyed – rightly or wrongly – that the USA was unwilling to intervene anywhere else, either. Her forces were cut back numerically and morally discredited in some influential circles. The Russian Politburo was not slow to probe this situation and become militarily involved in such diverse places as Angola, Ethiopia and Afghanistan – at first cautiously by proxy, but then with more direct Soviet intervention.

*President Carter working in the Oval Office at the time of his Camp David agreement between Israel and Egypt – a skilled piece of diplomacy that would become an important milestone on the road towards the ever-elusive peace in the Middle East. Carter actually gave the USA a more forward rôle in world affairs than his critics would subsequently allow; but he was badly wrong-footed at the end by the Iranian revolution.*

*American hostages being paraded on the first day of the Iranian occupation of the Tehran embassy, 4th November 1979. This incident seemed to symbolize all the wastefully powerless naïveté of US foreign policy during the seventeen years since the Cuban missile crisis.*

America's military response was initially confined to the procurement of sophisticated new weapons, especially the Cruise and MX Missiles, and the Space Shuttle. Arms race pressure against the USSR was thereby maintained through unmatchably advanced technology. A new Caribbean Task Force was also established, as was a globally-ranging Rapid Deployment Force. Both these measures enhanced the ability to project the power of the new zero-draft army to worldwide trouble spots. It would therefore be quite incorrect to see President Jimmy Carter's term of office, from 1976 to 1980, as an era of pacifism and passivity – even though he did admittedly discontinue both the B-1 bomber and the neutron bomb.

Carter's first and last military adventure was nevertheless a humiliating failure that the public found very hard to forgive. This came in response to the seizure of 66 US hostages in Tehran on 4th November 1979, just after the start of the Iran-Iraq Gulf War. By 24th April 1980, 53 of the hostages were still being held when a special Green Beret "Delta Force" unit mounted a complex but daring rescue bid.

The plan for Operation "Eagle Claw" was that eight RH-53D Sea Stallion helicopters would fly from USS *Nimitz* to a staging post in the desert – "Desert One" – where they would rendezvous with C-130s flying in from Egypt, via Oman, with fuel replenishment and an assault spearhead of 132 men including 93 Delta Force troops. Six helicopters – and no less than six were deemed necessary to make the operation viable – would then continue with the commandos to a hide site 50 miles from Tehran, called "Desert Two." There the men would be provided with trucks to drive to the US embassy in the center of the city. Once there, they would breach the wall with explosives and storm the buildings holding the hostages. They would kill the guards and release the Americans. The party would then be picked up by four helicopters, while AC-130 Specter fixed wing gunships flew cover. A secondary team would free three additional hostages from the Foreign Ministry building. The whole party would next fly out to the nearby town of Manzariyeh, where a company of Rangers would have seized an abandoned airfield. The final evacuation, covered by a swarm of naval fighter-bombers, would take place in two C-141 Star Lifter transport planes.

There were a number of fall-back procedures to cover the eventuality that less than six helicopters would be available to lift everyone out of Tehran. In the event, however, all the helicopters arrived late at Desert One after a gruelling terrain-hugging night flight through dust clouds. Worse, the suspected mechanical failure of three out of the eight led to a decision to abort the whole mission. The machines, run by fitters and pilots who were unaccustomed to such unusual strains, and lacking the most modern navigation aids, just could not stand the pace. Then, as the first helicopter lifted out on its way home, it unhappily struck a C-130 transport plane and started a conflagration that left eight dead and several more wounded. Injury had been tragically added to insult.

Bureaucratic in-fighting, a fragmented chain of command and an entirely overblown paranoia about security had blighted Operation "Eagle Claw" from the start. Not enough of the key people were ever allowed to know enough about what was going on to bring the whole thing together properly, and tactical communications were effectively abandoned by the imposition of radio silence. The darkness, and the noise and the dust of Desert One, all led to command chaos. It did not help that each element in the attack had been trained separately, as a separate arm of the service, in different places and with different combat philosophies.

When President Ronald Reagan took office he was able to devote more money to defense than his predecessor, funding not just the space-based Strategic Defense Initiative (popularly known as "Star Wars") and the deployment of Cruise and Pershing missiles to Europe; but also a major expansion of the conventional armory and its long range lift capability. Reagan also seemed more ready to make at least small scale military interventions overseas, in places as widespread as El Salvador, Honduras and the Persian Gulf. In Nicaragua he backed a long proxy war by the Contras, and in 1986 he bombed Colonel Gaddafi of Libya. In 1982 he placed a marine peacekeeping force in Beirut and in the following year he reversed a communist *coup d'état* in Grenada. President George Bush, his successor, would maintain this general attitude by deployments to Panama in 1989 and, on a vastly greater scale, to Saudi Arabia in 1990. The Tehran hostage crisis had brought such painful reminders of the Vietnam humiliations that Americans wanted to feel their country was "walking tall" once again – although until Saudi Arabia they evidently did not wish for another large scale, open ended, commitment of troops.

In Beirut American and French forces were deployed to underpin the agreement between Israel and the PLO that followed the Israeli invasion of Lebanon in June 1982. The 32nd Marine Amphibious Unit (MAU) landed on 25th August, to interpose itself between the two sides as the PLO guerrillas withdrew. It succeeded admirably in this mission; but the many PLO and Shiite civilians left behind in Beirut now came under threat from Lebanese Christians, and from a returned Israeli presence, the moment the marines left the city on 14th September. Without an

impartial peacekeeping force on the ground, there was simply no guarantee of stability or security. In the event there was a cold blooded massacre of civilians by the Christian militias, in the Shabra and Shatilla camps, between 18th and 20th September. The outraged American reaction was to send the marines ashore yet again, this time in collaboration with British, French and Italian contingents.

The motive behind this deployment was actually to maintain the peace and prevent any repetition of the Shabra and Shatilla massacres. However, some widely differing perceptions of US intentions rapidly developed, depending on the viewpoint of the parties involved. This peacekeeping force became a very ambiguous

symbol to the people of Beirut, every bit as quickly as the British Army's peacekeeping force in Belfast had lost its originally intended "neutral" image in 1969-70. At initially 1,200 men, furthermore, 32nd MAU (later replaced in rotation by 24th and 22nd MAU) scarcely amounted to an overwhelming counterweight to Israeli and Syrian forces in Lebanon, which at this time still ran into many divisions. Even by the end of the commitment, US personnel in the entire region would number no more than 14,000, with less than 2,000 on the ground. This contrasts sharply with more than 70,000 deployed to Saudi Arabia within a few weeks in August 1990.

The problem for the Americans in Beirut seems to have been that they simply lacked the numbers needed to grip the situation in the way it really demanded. To have deployed such numbers would have involved the USA in "another Vietnam," which was still politically unacceptable. Indeed, it is highly relevant to mention that Israel herself has now come to regard her own deployment to Lebanon in 1982-3 as equivalent to "Israel's Vietnam." It was every bit as costly, frustrating and fruitless as the earlier conflict, and led to equivalent domestic divisions.

As 1982 passed into 1983 the marines in Beirut found they could get on well with the Shiite population local to their positions; but they increasingly found themselves coming under fire from all sides – from the Israeli Defense Force as well as from Islamic fundamentalists. The more diplomatic peace feelers and arms shipments were extended towards the Christians and Israelis, however, the more the USA began to be tagged with an "anti Moslem" image. On 18th April the American embassy was bombed, resulting in 17 US and 40 other deaths. On 22nd July the marine positions began to be shelled, and a straightforward local battle soon developed

ABOVE LEFT

*In Operation Eagle Claw, April 1980, the inability of US armed forces to rescue the Tehran hostages showed that it was not only the politicians who still had lessons to learn from the Vietnam experience. Here Iranian officials inspect the grisly remains at "Desert One."*

LEFT

*President Ronald Reagan in the Oval Office at the end of 1987. As Carter's successor, it had fallen to him to restore American pride and make the country feel it could "walk tall" in the world once again. In fact, however, his overseas military adventures were often relatively small scale and tentative, despite their tonic effect on public opinion.*

between the Islamic Druse militia and American land, sea and air forces. US neutrality had by this time entirely evaporated in all but name.

The most shocking act in this war came on 23rd October, when a Moslem suicide bomber accelerated his truckload of explosives through flimsy obstacles right into the lobby of the marine headquarters, and blew it apart, killing 241 Americans and injuring a further 71 in one of the most spectacular and lethal acts of terrorism of all time. It was immediately followed by a similar attack on the French barracks, where there was a total of 73 casualties, and then by an attack on an Israeli outpost. As a response to these events there was a grim series of retaliatory strikes by US, French and Israeli forces, but they achieved very little. On 30th March 1984 President Reagan cut his losses, which by now totalled 372 casualties, and declared that the US forces were going home.

A measure of national prestige was nevertheless salvaged in Operation "Urgent Fury" mounted on 25th October 1983, just two days after the Beirut massacre. This was the invasion of Grenada, designed to reverse both the growing influence of Cuba in the island and a recent leftist coup led by General Hudson Austin. It was also a substantial political success for the Reagan administration insofar as it assured the safety of almost 1,000 US medical students – thereby warding off a potential hostage crisis that could have become embarrassingly reminiscent of Tehran in 1979-80. In 1990 President George Bush would be faced with a much tougher dilemma over the many more US citizens detained in Iraq.

Another refreshing feature of the Grenada operation was that – unlike earlier involvements in Vietnam and Lebanon – it enjoyed a large measure of encouragement from closely-involved friendly states; in this case Antigua, Barbados, Dominica, Jamaica, St. Lucia, St. Vincent and St. Kitts. The British found it difficult to endorse North American action in the island – a member

*Marines come ashore over the beaches near Beirut's international airport at the end of September 1982. This second peace-keeping intervention within a month was prompted by chilling massacres at the Sabra and Shatilla refugee camps.*

RIGHT

*Marines patrolling Beirut in November 1982. The aim was to dampen violence between warring factions, but US numbers were never large enough to be really effective, and the political landscape itself kept changing with bewildering rapidity.*

of the Commonwealth and still technically ruled by the Queen – since it cut directly across their own long-term local policies. Pro-Reagan Prime Minister Margaret Thatcher was nevertheless mindful of generous US assistance in resisting the 1982 South American invasion of some other Commonwealth islands – the Falklands – and chose to turn a blind eye in this case. The whole episode contrasted starkly with US peacekeeping operations in Lebanon, where they had always been hamstrung by intense political divisions, not just between the factions within the country, but especially between the many powerful nation-states that were also involved. In Vietnam, yet again, President Johnson's repeated attempts to "Call in more flags" to support the operation had always been far less successful than he had hoped, especially among NATO members. Before Grenada it had thus been only the Korean War that had seen a truly encouraging international response to a US appeal for "more flags."

Despite all these political factors working in favor of Operation "Urgent Fury," it was, nevertheless, somewhat flawed as a military action. As had already happened too often in Vietnam, and then in the Iran rescue attempt, there was imperfect coordination between the Army, Air Force, Navy and Marines. Each service had its own standard operating procedures and perspectives, making unified command difficult. These complexities were not reduced by the addition of Army Delta Force and Navy Seal teams conducting a number of special operations, with two Army Ranger battalions in support, all under the command of a headquarters that was organizationally separate from that of the main force.

Unfortunately the overnight Delta Force attempt to seize Point Salines airfield, on the southwestern tip of the island, was a failure that served only to alert the island's garrison. The next

*A marine with M-16 rifle grenade launcher stands guard over the shattered US embassy in Beirut. A bomb destroyed part of the building on 18th April 1983, causing scores of casualties. Unfortunately, this was not to be the last bomb attack on American installations in the city.*

*On 23rd October 1983 a suicide bomber destroyed the US Marine headquarters in Beirut, causing about twice as many casualties in a single moment as were lost in the entire Gulf War of 1991. This tragic incident signalled the beginning of the end for President Reagan's Beirut policy.*

Delta Force assault, intended to free political prisoners from the jail at the nearby capital, St. George's, thus came under heavy fire while it was still in its helicopters, and that attack was aborted. Nor did the smaller Seal missions enjoy much better success, since three out of four of them fell short of achieving their objectives. After this there was a parachute drop on Point Salines airfield by two very under strength, hence over commanded, battalions of the 75th Rangers. The drop had to be improvised while actually in the air, since the original plan had been to land after Delta Force had cleared the runway. Parachutes had to be used when the runway could not be cleared; but fire from the alerted enemy caused confusion in both the drop itself and in the reorganization on the ground. Only half the runway could be opened to a landing by elements of 82nd Airborne Division by 2 pm; but when this took place it was still being brought under enemy fire. It would not be until the following morning that the entire airfield area could be considered truly secure, and the first batch of US students was flown home rejoicing.

Meanwhile the 1-84th Marine Amphibious Group had successfully seized Pearls airport on the east side of the island, including a landing by armor from the sea. However, the marines were now called upon to reembark most of their force to assist the bogged advance of the lightly-armed 82nd Airborne into the St. George's area. They achieved this with great speed and precision, thereby demonstrating that amphibious assault ships possess considerably more tactical flexibility than large fixed-wing transport planes which require immovable runways. Indeed, their champions would also suggest that the entire operation should have been entrusted to the Marine Corps from the start, rather than be allowed to descend into the morass of conflicting inter-service command responsibilities that it actually did.

There remained three days of messy mopping-up operations in which additional American battalions were trickled into the battle area until a total of around 7,000 men were on the ground. The total US casualty list rose to approximately 180, as opposed to perhaps 500 Grenadians and Cubans – most of whom were apparently civilians. These three days also included the extraction of some 426 students who had embarrassingly escaped intelligence notice until the initial group was rescued. It seems that the enemy had been allowed a very ample opportunity to turn its guns against them, had it wished to do so; fortunately it did not. Thus the underlying irony of the Grenada attack is that it had in part been intended to demonstrate the government's ability to rescue hostages, yet from a technical, military point of view it actually conveyed the opposite message. It is only because the Grenadian and Cuban

garrison was relatively humanely disposed towards its American student guests that a bloodbath was avoided; not because of US military action. Even the Ayatollah Khomeni in 1979-80 had stopped short of murdering his American hostages, when he could have done so, albeit less from motives of humanity than from a studied political calculation.

The worry with all this, of course, is that in a future conflict the hostage-taker may not prove to be so open to considerations of either humanity or rationality. In such a case the USA would suddenly be forced to come eyeball to eyeball with a set of ethical and political dilemmas that would be considerably more unwelcome and painful than anything encountered in either Vietnam or Tehran. In the political and journalistic conditions of the modern world it seems that a determined hostage taker can wield almost as much deterrence – or "blackmail" – as the possessor of strategic nuclear weapons. We may even today be entering an entirely new era of history, in which it will no longer be the task of armed forces to retaliate against damaging hostile strikes like Pearl Harbor, nor to recapture lost territory such as the Argonne or Ardenne forests. Instead, the aim may increasingly be to release innocent hostages before they can be harmed by an aggressor.

*Operation Urgent Fury was launched in Grenada just two days after the Beirut massacre, bringing a needed success to American arms. Inter-service rivalries, however, created avoidable command and control overlaps. They would be smoothed out in the Goldwater-Nichols Defense Reorganization Act of 1985, making things easier in the Middle East five years later.*

LEFT

*Armored carriers patrol the streets of St George's, Grenada, four days after the invasion. The city had baffled initial attempts to seize it, but had soon fallen to a flexible amphibious switch of Marine armor from one invasion beach to another.*

ABOVE RIGHT

*Marines holding suspected members of the People's Revolutionary Army, 28th October 1983, in St George's, Grenada. In the event it took several days longer to control the situation and free all the US hostages than had originally been hoped.*

President Reagan's reputation for tough action, in Grenada, and again in Libya on 15th May 1986, was based more on his political willingness to use military force than on the surgical precision of that force itself. In the late 1980s the hope had to be that the armed services would be able to learn from the past and adapt themselves to the new types of mission they were now most likely to face. For example, four new "Light Divisions" were coming forward for rapid deployment to low intensity conflicts, and a lively debate about their possible tactics was under way. The first key test of all this would come on 20th December 1989, when President George Bush launched Operation "Just Cause" to topple President Manuel Antonio Noriega of Panama.

In Panama there was the enormous advantage that the operation's startline was a secure, well-supplied, long-established US base from which there was direct overland access to the objective. This contrasts with every US military action since at least 1945, and probably since the 1914 Mexican involvement. Nevertheless, in 1989 the lesson had certainly been learned that overwhelmingly large forces had to be introduced into the battlezone right at the very start – not trickled in gradually, a few at a time, as in Grenada. In Panama 24,000 men went into action almost together, creating an impression of hopelessness in the minds of the defenders and thereby minimizing hostilities.

There were also some impressive tactical successes, in part stemming from reforms in the chain of command following the Grenada experience. Since the Goldwater-Nichols Defense Reorganization Act of 1985, great strides forward had been made in unifying the hierarchy and planning of each expeditionary force under the Joint Chiefs of Staff. This avoided the earlier "salad bowl" approach, in which each service had seen itself as a quasi-autonomous entity.

In the Arraijan and La Chorrera areas the US marines achieved excellent results clearing road blocks and defended buildings with their new Fleet Anti-terrorism Security Team (FAST). These elite commandos benefited from accurate covering fire from 25mm cannon mounted on wheeled Light Armor Vehicles (LAV's) and 152 mm guns on air-dropped M551 Sheridan airborne reconnaissance assault vehicles. At the Rio Hato airfield US Rangers had to fight a hard house-to-house battle against a half battalion of Noriega's elite US-trained troops, but they secured the area in less than an hour. At Fort Amador a very precise artillery strike demolished the enemy barracks without causing collateral damage.

Elsewhere the first battle commanded by a female commissioned officer was a distinct success. Neverthless there were some tragic cases of what leading strategist Edward N. Luttwak has called "the manifestly frivolous use of weapons of all kinds." The tempting availability of awesome firepower sometimes led to its use in inappropriate situations, including the leveling of several apartment blocks – and the death of their inhabitants – in Panama City. Nor was Noriega himself initially arrested, but had to be run to earth in an embarrassingly protracted manhunt that ended in a bombardment by amplified pop music of his refuge in the papal embassy!

Panama did at least show that President Bush was prepared to send larger forces into action than had either of his two predecessors. This was partly because he was able to profit from their preliminary work in doubling the available deployable forces, and partly a result of the general easing of East-West tensions. Since the Korean War Pentagon planners had always had to cover their backs in Germany before they could divert sizeable resources to other theaters; but this was now becoming a much less important factor. By August 1990 Bush certainly felt able to go very much further even than in Panama, when he ordered Operation "Desert Shield" to protect Saudi Arabia against possible Iraqi aggression. A startling total of 70,000 Americans – over half of them marines – was initially committed to this deployment, and the Reserve was called out for the first time since the Tet offensive of 1968. In addition, a gratifyingly large number of foreign contingents responded to the call for "more flags." The whole proposition looked as though it could easily turn into the biggest American war since Vietnam. This perception was to be more than confirmed during the months that followed, as the US component of the allied force rapidly rose to more than 500,000 personnel within a total coalition deployment of around three quarters of a million.

RIGHT

*Central America was in many ways the focus of President Reagan's military attention, due to his determination to prevent communist infiltration through Uncle Sam's back door. Scandal, however, would adhere to some of the schemes to support Nicaraguan Contra rebels such as this one – whose rusty old RPD M-53 Russian machine gun clearly needs replacing.*

ABOVE

A major political difficulty with counter-insurgency campaigning in Central America was that it looked and smelt too much like Vietnam. Here two Oregon National Guardsmen exercise alongside a Honduran paratrooper, using the same type of Huey helicopter that had been ubiquitous in the Indochina conflict.

LEFT

Men of 82nd Airborne Division land at Palmerola, Honduras, from a C-141 of the strategic airlift, 17th March 1988. Note the new "German style" helmets.

An airborne Sheridan light tank, "Big Duke 2," is made ready for joint operations with the Honduran army, 18th March 1988. As Nicaragua's next door neighbor, Honduras needed protection against retaliation for the Contras' cross-border raiding.

RIGHT

The OV-1 Mohawk surveillance aircraft had proved its value in counter-insurgency operations in Vietnam. Here it takes off to scan the Nicaraguan border as 82nd Airborne paratroopers wait for the flight home from Honduras.

ABOVE

US Secretary of State James Baker sees eye to eye with reforming Soviet leader Mikhail Gorbachev in Moscow, May 1989, as the Cold War draws to its close. It would not take long for the USA to start flexing its global muscles as the only remaining superpower.

LEFT

Gorbachev points the way forward to Fidel Castro in Havana, April 1989. The veteran Cuban leader seems to be making a rather different point, but is unable to prevent growing US interventionism in Central America.

TOP

President Manuel Antonio Noriega of Panama waves to supporters after foiling an attempted military coup against him that did not win US support.

ABOVE

Noriega's security troops of "Battalion 2,000," using a mixture of Russian and American equipment, keep the road closed outside defense headquarters, October 1989.

*President George Bush launched Operation Just Cause to liberate Panama, on a wide front and with overwhelmingly strong forces, on 20th December 1989. Here some of the prisoners arrive at the detention camp near Panama City two days later.*

ABOVE

The futuristic F117A Stealth Fighter was first used in combat during the Panama invasion. Its jagged lines are designed to eat up incoming radar waves, thus decreasing the profile seen on the enemy's screen. Against the unsophisticated defenses encountered in Just Cause, however, it is doubtful that such elaborate and expensive precautions were really necessary. The stealth fighter would come much more into its true element during the air war over Iraq, 1991.

ABOVE RIGHT

Great collateral damage was caused in the Chorrillo district of Panama City, where these civilian dwellings were accidentally flattened during the attack, causing great loss of life.

*Prison photograph of ex-President Noriega, released by the US Attorney's office, Miami, on 4th January 1990. The Panama invasion had been mounted to bring him to trial for drug trafficking, although it was noticeable that Operation Desert Storm a year later would have no such personal war aims. Uncle Sam is apparently forced to pay greater attention to the international proprieties when he plays far from home than when he plays in his own back yard.*

ABOVE

*A shoe shine provides a welcome break from duties during Operation Just Cause.*

# CHAPTER TEN

# TEAM YANKEE AND NATO'S DEFENSE OF GERMANY

*Technologies, prospects and threats for the US ground forces of the future*

Every President since Franklin D. Roosevelt has made some sort of emergency military deployment to the Third World, yet since 1943 America's largest field army has almost always been found in Europe. During the period of the Cold War, the US Seventh Army in Germany was built up to around a third of a million men, with some 5,000 tanks, supported by a complex defended line of communication stretching all the way back across the Atlantic. In the event of war, a further million troops would be lifted in, alongside most of the available tactical airpower. This reinforcement has been regularly practised, for example in Operation "Crested Cap" for the Air Force and, since 1968, in Operation "Reforger" for dual-based ground formations. If such deployments actually had to be undertaken, they would make the overnight 1972 shift of hundreds of aircraft from training in California to combat in Vietnam look like a very minor exercise by comparison; and even the 1990 Operation "Desert Shield" would be dwarfed.

BELOW LEFT

*The Berlin Wall, built in 1961, can just be seen through NATO barbed wire at the famous Brandenburg Gate. The defense of West Berlin and West Germany would be the top priority for US military policy between 1948 and 1990, and the great triumph of those years has been that it never came to a shooting war.*

BELOW

*Major General Albert Watson II, US Berlin commandant, returns through Checkpoint Charlie after visiting the Soviet commandant, October 1961. Tensions were running especially high at this time, and the visit had been to protest at increased restrictions on American access to East Berlin.*

The battle for Germany loomed especially large in US military thinking during the years between the collapse of South Vietnam in 1975 and the end of the Cold War in 1990. The Vietnam conflict had helped point the way towards many new technologies for conventional warfare; but the relatively low intensity of the fighting there had often hindered their adaptation to the tactics of "the big league." Once the troops had come home from Vietnam and the Army had been restructured, there was a new-found freedom to explore these avenues.

The first attempt to apply the lessons of Vietnam to Germany was the 1976 version of Army Field Manual *100-5 Operations*. This envisaged a battle in which US forces would be thinly stretched in a defensive line facing numerically greatly superior Warsaw Pact armored thrusts. The concept of "Active Defense" would be used, whereby forces not immediately engaged by main enemy spearheads would be maneuvered to reinforce sections of the line that were. Threatened points could thus be bolstered up to a level of firepower sufficient to impose heavy losses on the enemy so that the more he advanced, the more he would be punished. Even if final victory could not be offered by these means, there would still be a major deterrent effect.

Active Defense depended on advanced mathematical modeling that determined just how many weapons would be needed to "service each target," or in other words to achieve an adequate level of attrition against each enemy unit. With

ABOVE RIGHT

*The 1970s doctrine of "Active Defense" already rested on a new generation of high technology firepower weapons, although these would not be tested in combat until the Gulf War of 1991. One example is this Multiple Launch Rocket System, a sophisticated divisional support weapon that enhances the basic idea behind the "Stalin's Organ" used to great effect by the Red Army during WW2. Later versions of this weapon are designed to fire "smart" rockets with pinpoint accuracy to as much as 30 miles' range.*

RIGHT

*The AH-64 Apache attack helicopter, successor to the Huey Cobra "Snake" of Vietnam notoriety, was designed with Warsaw Pact tanks and anti-aircraft fire very much in mind. It especially proved itself in Kuwait, 1991, with its thermal sights, high tactical agility, and potent cluster of HE rockets, Hellfire anti-tank missiles and 30 mm chain gun.*

LEFT

*One lesson of Vietnam that was imported into the European theater in the 1970s was the need for a close support aircraft that could fly low and slow over the front line. This need was met by the A-10 "Warthog" tank-buster: an essentially simple aircraft that sacrificed high performance for heavy armor and a powerful punch with GAU-8/A Avenger rotary cannon, and smart bombs.*

new weapons coming forward in the 1970s and 1980s, the Army's tacticians found some exciting possibilities for combining precision guided weapons with self propelled artillery fire and electronically-directed air strikes. And just around the corner was a new generation of long range rockets that could dispense showers of homing bomblets (called "smartlets") onto the tops of enemy tanks.

The critics of Active Defense nevertheless detected all too many elements within it that were depressingly familiar from Vietnam. It seemed to be less a case of learning from past mistakes than of repeating them. In particular, the general posture seemed entirely defensive and based on firepower and attrition – an approach that had been increasingly discredited ever since General Westmoreland had been prohibited from making hot pursuits into Laos and Cambodia. In neither case had there apparently been a clear concept of how a final victory might be won. By stripping units from "quiet" parts of the line, furthermore, Active Defense seemed to be repeating the Vietnam habit of abandoning ground to the enemy as soon as it had been won. Hence the "Active" part of "Active Defense" soon began to look like a euphemism for a very passive posture indeed, and the outnumbered US line in Germany came to be represented as a gigantic repetition of the thin US line that had tried to hold South Vietnam.

In 1982 the Army issued a new edition of Field Manual 100-5, completely changing its whole doctrine and posture in a more genuinely

aggressive direction. This was based on an analysis by Vietnam armor expert General Donn A. Starry, who was now head of the Training and Doctrine Command (TRADOC). His starting point was the finding that 1970s Soviet tactics depended on an echelonment of attacking forces in great depth, with each assault regiment backed up by a second echelon regiment; each assault division by a second echelon division – and so on right up to the level of "Fronts" – ie groups of armies.

In response to his perception of the Soviet threat, Starry's key concept was "The Extended Battlefield," whereby incoming enemy spearheads would be destroyed by being cut off from their supporting second echelons advancing from the rear. Armor and airborne infantry would maneuver and attack behind the enemy first echelon, supported by deep air and artillery strikes. Enemy second echelons would be delayed and harassed for a critical timespan before they could enter the immediate battle area. This would isolate ("interdict") the front line battle so that it could be won at leisure by friendly forces. In 1984 General Bernard Rogers, the Supreme Allied Commander in Europe, would endorse much of this thinking by his doctrine of Follow On Forces Attack ("FOFA").

Starry's Extended Battlefield certainly did not represent a rejection of technology, since it depended on such futuristic devices as deeply-deployed electronic sensors and airborne (manned or unmanned) platforms that could relay realtime lookdown surveillance to ground commanders.

Some of the deep strikes would be made by the "Assault Breaker" package of long range anti-armor rocket munitions guided to their targets by secure radio loops from the surveillance assets. Permeating the whole doctrine, in fact, was a sense of the exciting possibilities that the newly Emerging Technology ("ET") could now offer. Behind this lay an enthusiasm for a family of less exotic, but still highly advanced, new weapons that were just arriving in the Army's inventory: such items as the Blackhawk and Apache helicopters; the A-10 armored anti-tank ground attack aircraft; the MLRS "smart" improvement on the famed Russian Katushya multiple rocket launcher; the Bradley infantry fighting vehicle, and the astonishingly agile M-1 General Abrams tank. Perhaps even the choice of this last name, rather than that of General Westmoreland, betrayed a sub-conscious belief that the old attritional approaches were now being changed..

Despite all the technological excitement underlying FM 100-5/1982, there was also a sticking point. The manual had to deal with the Army as it actually was; not with how it might look in twenty years time, when every problem could presumably be solved at the touch of a button. The new doctrine therefore did not go anything like as far into futuristic technological speculation as some other operational discussions of the same time – notably the 1981 TRADOC paper entitled *AirLand Battle 2000*. Whereas the latter looked forward to really long range conventional munitions with pinpoint accuracy at 300 kilometers, FM 100-5 limited itself to a battle fought mainly within a more easily attainable zone around 50 km ahead of friendly positions. It also contained a very significant "anti-technological" emphasis on traditional military virtues such as military spirit, maneuver and close combat. Starry's armored and airmobile soldiers were expected to go out and take the war to the enemy, seizing the initiative in a fast-moving battle of cut and thrust. There would no longer be a passive calculus of attrition and defense, but a new willingness to counter-attack.

In the specific case of Operation "Desert Storm" in 1991, for example, it was not enough merely to stand in defense of Saudi Arabia when the true *casus belli* had been the loss of Kuwait. The doctrine of "taking the war to the enemy" meant that Saddam Hussein had to be kicked out of his conquests – and disarmed within his own territory in Southern Iraq – in a way that had so obviously not happened in Laos, Cambodia and North Vietnam between 1965 and 1973.

The new conventional warfare doctrines of the early 1980s also led to a re-examination of the details of tactics. Combat assaults by helicopter, for example, were revised to take account of the much heavier air defense weapons that might be encountered in Europe. Instead of relying on a few scout helicopters and gunships for support, the infantry transporters would now be able to call on sophisticated electronic counter-measure helicopters and terminally-homing flak suppression munitions. They would act in task groups sweeping SAM-free corridors, just like the fixed wing air force. Indeed, a judicious mix of ground forces with fixed- and rotary-wing aircraft would now co-operate together as never before, to their mutual benefit. For example the Israeli invasion of Lebanon in 1982 had demonstrated the importance of remotely piloted vehicles in finding enemy SAMs, tracking them in real time, and decoying their fire. The Soviet war in Afghanistan, however, had shown the power of the Hind D helicopter gunship, and had added a worrying new dimension to the problem. In future conflicts American helicopter forces would have to be ready to engage ground targets at the same time as they fought air-to-air dogfights against enemy helicopters

Something similar could be said of tanks, which learned to fight as a team not just with helicopters, but also with a new breed of armored infantry that rode in purpose-built combat vehicles developed from the improvised "ACAVs" of Vietnam. Studies of the Arab-Israeli October war of 1973 had underlined the importance of moving earth to protect tanks, so each M-I Abrams was to be accompanied by its own armored bulldozer. Equally the 1973 war had shown the limitations of wire guided anti tank missiles such as the Soviet-made Sagger. Although this was admittedly a less efficient weapon than the American TOW, it was still felt that a new generation of "fire and forget" missiles, such as Hellfire, was urgently needed. The race became still more acute after the Israeli operations of 1982, during which new laminated armor and (explosive) reactive armor plates had been demonstrated. The new armors were also ominously observed on the new Soviet T80 tanks, threatening to make all NATO anti-tank missiles obsolete at a stroke. Yet another new generation of missiles had to be designed, to assure continuing penetration.

During the mid-1980s fear of the Warsaw Pact

continued to run high, not merely because of its advances in technology, but also because its assault doctrines seemed to have shifted away from the deeply-echeloned formations that Starry had assumed. The latest Soviet thinking called for a "single echelon" or "standing start" attack, in which even relatively light spearheads would crash through the NATO front line before it had been alerted, and would race deep into the heart of Germany to win the war by surprise before it had properly begun. Such a *coup de main* would not require any follow-on echelons until after the battle was over. It would not be vulnerable to deep interdiction, so some improvements in Western responsiveness and maneuver thinking were apparently required.

Part of the answer emerged from a new system of combat training and analysis. In the past, many of the Army's ideas about the nature of battle had originated in the time-honored techniques of the arms salesman, the combat veteran, the historian, the Moscow-watcher, and especially of the engineer and the mathematical operations researcher. A veritable boom town of technical consultancies and think tanks had sprung up around Washington to service the Pentagon. In 1981, however, the Army added a new facility of its own to the analytical repertoire, when it opened the National Training Center ("NTC") in the high Mojave desert in California. This was a combat simulator on a gigantic scale, in which real US armored regiments could maneuver against a mocked-up Warsaw Pact force, firing laser guns against enemy vehicles and men fitted with special designators. A hit of the right type would immobilize the target and compel the enemy commander to adjust his plans accordingly.

The beauty of the NTC system was that it appeared to be impartial and completely fair, since the laser guns so accurately replicated the hit probabilities of real tank cannon, rocket launchers and rifles. There was none of the reliance upon subjective umpires that had tended to make "free play" exercises unconvincing or questionable in the past. Secondly, the "enemy" forces were configured to operate in conformity with Warsaw Pact doctrines, and their vehicles were given comparable physical profiles. Best of all, the entire "enemy" team was made up of permanent residents at the NTC, who enjoyed a complete mastery of their job. Whenever a green US unit came into action against them, it was taught vital combat lessons in the school of hard knocks.

Most peacetime soldiers passing through the NTC are astounded by the rigors of its demands. Mistakes are punished pitilessly, and combat

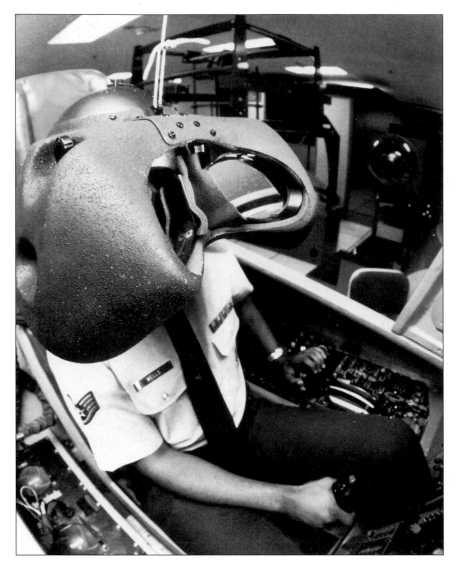

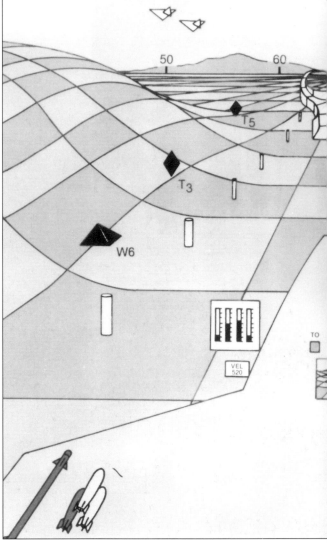

commands wither away with frightening rapidity under the fire of a "live" enemy. In a sense this undermines confidence and emphasizes the mortality of tanks and men on the modern battlefield. It is certainly noticeable that the (surprisingly many) fictionalized accounts that have come out of the NTC have been marked by a somewhat morbid vision of lines of tanks and infantry vehicles brewing up and burning furiously after receiving just a few seconds of enemy fire. Harold Coyle's *Team Yankee*, for example, paints a pitiless picture of a Third World War battlefield in which the dead outnumber wounded and prisoner casualties to a degree previously quite unknown in modern warfare. NTC training is obviously not designed to create complacency among armored soldiers, and seems to stress the idea that modern armored combat is a very dangerous game to play.

Yet against this influence must be set the higher success of the NTC in imparting professionalism and confidence – almost over-confidence – in most of its alumni. They feel that they have "been there" and have "seen the elephant" of war in a way that was unattainable in any previous training programs–apart perhaps from "battle inoculation" exercises that willingly accepted real casualties to live firing. The NTC graduates will certainly have improved their skills in armored warfare and will go away thinking deeply about it, even if they have not quite savored the special private insight that is bestowed only to the genuine combat veteran. Coyle's *Team Yankee* armored force did finally win its battle, after all.

By 1990 the United States had solidly re-built the regiments that had been shaken by Vietnam and the military restructuring that followed. She had devoted an unprecedented effort to the study of conventional warfare operations and now, with President Mikhail Gorbachev's rapid reforms in Eastern Europe, she was once more free to project power globally on a large scale in defence of Western Interests. History had come full circle, and President Bush's forces that went into action so effectively in the Gulf were every bit as confident, well armed and combat-ready as the marines who first landed at Da Nang in 1965, or the doughboys who finished off the First World War by fighting their way through the Argonne Forest.

ABOVE LEFT

*"Emerging Technology" (ET) extends beyond the hardware of rockets and airplanes into the very brains of their operators. This experimental Visually Coupled Airborne System Simulator allows a pilot to fly without having to touch any controls or look outside the aircraft. All the data he needs is projected onto a screen within the helment, and his intended maneuvers are registered by voice or movements of his eyes or head.*

ABOVE

*An advanced visual display system designed to present pilots with all the information they need on a single screen. Aircraft status, fuel and weapons are shown towards the bottom of the screen, while the projected flight path is the twisting track at the center. Along the route potential threats are highlighted, including enemy radars, SAMs and airplanes.*

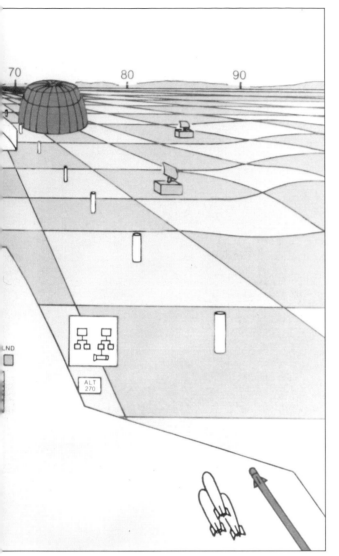

*Enthusiasm for ET weapons was boosted during the Reagan years by the still more advanced technologies being studied for the Strategic Defense Initiative (or "Star Wars"). Pictured here is an artist's impression of "The Swarm" concept for multiple phased array target acquisition satellites. The spin-off from such space-based concepts is gradually being felt nearer to the ground, for example in the Patriot anti-aircraft missile that was used with success against Scud ballistic missiles in 1991.*

*The Aerospace Plane, a proposed successor to the Space Shuttle that would utilize revolutionary materials and propulsion systems. Such vehicles would make it easier to place SDI equipment in space, although the price tag still seems to be prohibitive.*

LEFT AND ABOVE

*A freelance attempt to destroy the Berlin Wall was made on 17th April 1963 by an East German mechanic driving a stolen armored car. A police construction team is here repairing the damage, and it would be 26 long years before the cranes were brought back to finally tear down the wall and reunite Germany.*

BELOW

*The Army's most advanced tank, the M-1 Abrams, was the focus of many new maneuver-based doctrines developed during the 1980s. It is seen here exercising in the Saudi Arabian desert in September 1990; but apart from the camels the terrain bears close similarities the NTC's high Mojave Desert in California. The NTC thus made an important preparation for victory in 1991.*

# CHAPTER ELEVEN

# THE DESERT SHIELD AND THE DESERT STORM

When Iraq invaded Kuwait on 2nd August 1990, she triggered the biggest US military response since Vietnam – and actually a far faster and more technically powerful one. Whereas it took the best part of three years to put some 600,000 lightly-equipped 'counter-insurgency' troops into Southeast Asia during the mid-1960s, in late 1990 it took just five months to put almost the same number of heavy conventional warfare troops into the Gulf. If the new conflict was planned in accordance with the 'lessons of Vietnam', therefore, perhaps its most striking achievement was the sheer speed and scale of the initial deployment in Operation *Desert Shield*.

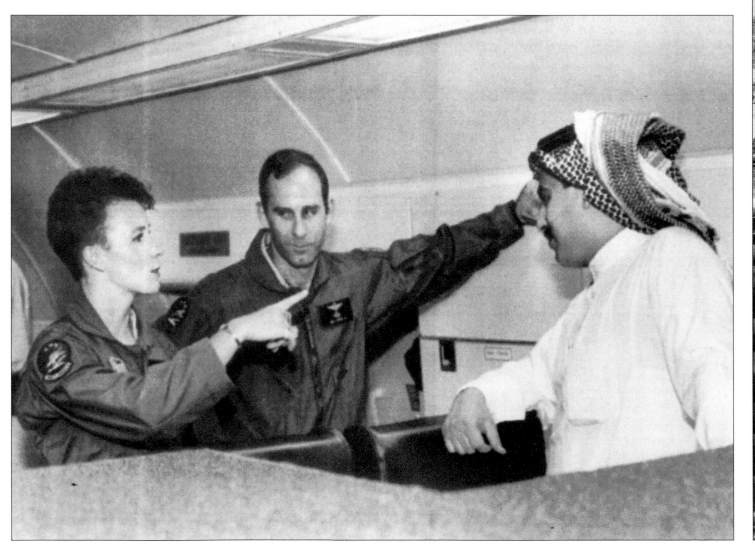

A Saudi Arabian government representative finds that the USAF AWACs aircraft defending his country have female as well as male crew members. This would never be allowed under the strict Saudi Islamic laws, but it did not stop the AWACS from vectoring Saudi pilots onto their targets with high precision during the war.

Marines reinforce their bunkers with sandbags during their initial deployment in Operation Desert Shield, August 1990. They were aware at the time that fewer US forces had arrived than the press was telling the world, so they would have been vulnerable to a major Iraqi thrust if one had been launched at that time.

The deployment was doubly impressive since the decision to go for it at all had been taken with only very short prior warning. There had not been the long years of build-up within the region that had been seen in Vietnam, and during the first few weeks of deployment only a relatively weak, token force could be put on the ground. This could have been overrun by a concerted Iraqi attack at that time, had it not been portrayed as far more powerful than it actually was. In his first skilled exploitation of the media – and arguably also the most vital one – General H. Norman Schwarzkopf, overall US commander in the theater, successfully bluffed the Iraqis into inaction. By the time they had realized the extent of the deception, sufficient coalition firepower had arrived for them to be genuinely deterred from further aggression.

The 'cold start' to *Desert Shield* was at least mitigated by the many feasibility studies that had been made, ever since the Shah's overthrow in 1979, into a large military deployment to the deserts of Iran. President Carter had already started preparing the logistic and organizational base for such a deployment, including greatly improved diplomatic and military relations with Saudi Arabia and Egypt – and his successor had carried those preparations still further forward. In that sense *Desert Shield* had not been totally unplanned, since many of its vital features had been carefully worked out on paper in the Pentagon. Some of them will be immediately recognizable to readers of Harold Coyle's 1988 novel *Sword Point* – a neatly fictionalized presentation of the 'Iran' scenario, as well as of the desert warfare training purveyed at the NTC.

The wider military-diplomatic problem encountered in Kuwait was also in some ways very familiar. Just as she had in both Vietnam and Korea, America was once again trying to save a friendly nation from occupation by a heavily- (and largely Soviet-) armed neighbour which had a population of around 18 million. The US military had learned a number of lessons from these earlier experiences and knew, for example, that it should neither respect the enemy's sanctuaries too strictly (as in Indochina), nor pursue him too far over his border (as in Korea). In the Kuwait Theater of Operations (KTO) the assault would therefore spill far over the Kuwait border into Iraq itself, but would stop short of a drive on Baghdad. It would be a 'hot pursuit' without becoming a diplomatically embarrassing over-extension.

Whereas Korea had been hilly and Vietnam heavily afforested, the KTO had the advantage of being largely a flat, sandy desert devoid of cover. It was in many ways the ideal 'Free Fire Area' in which the ideal US weapon mix could be properly deployed. The full panoply of advanced armored warfare could be arrayed there in a way that had

not been possible in either Vietnam or Korea, and it could be supported by an air force unshackled by half-hearted theories of graduated action. In the year of German unification, moreover, the State Department did not have to be cautious through fear of communist strength in Europe – especially since in February 1991 a date would even be set for the abolition of the Warsaw Pact itself. In these circumstances President Bush felt he could take away most of the fighting power from 7th Army in Germany, in order to bolster the forces in the Gulf.

Iraq's lines of communication between Kuwait and Baghdad were also far easier to cut than the Ho Chi Minh Trail had ever been, especially since the technology of air to ground warfare had advanced mightily by 1991. The air interdiction of Saddam Hussein's ground forces could thus be modeled not on the failed 1960s Operations Ig*loo White* and *Rolling Thunder*, but on the successful

*Linebacker 1* of spring 1972 (when Hanoi's conventional ground attack was stopped dead in its tracks by air power) and on *Linebacker 2* of December 1972 (when central Hanoi itself was finally blitzed with remarkably light US aircraft losses).

All this meant President Bush could give a solemn promise that the new war would not be like Vietnam, in a number of different ways. Firstly, he was promising to cut through political complexities and unite the whole world behind American leadership. This was the moment at which the USA would forcibly demonstrate it was the sole remaining superpower, alone capable of reviving the flagging United Nations. She would rally support to the justice of her cause, both at home and abroad, very much as she had in WW2 and Korea. During much of the Cold War this stance had been compromised by the ideological division of the UN between the Western and

*General H. Norman Schwarzkopf, known affectionately as "The Bear," was overall commander of US forces in the Gulf. From the very start of deployment in August 1990 he employed a team of high-profile personal bodyguards, doubtless already believing himself to be the invaluable military asset that the public has subsequently agreed he is.*

*A Marine lands in Saudi Arabia complete with her emergency water supply and bulky chemical warfare protection kit. Neither types of equipment were to play as great a role as originally expected during Operation Desert Storm, since it often rained and the Iraqis did not, after all, resort to gas warfare.*

Eastern blocs, but that no longer applied. The way was clear for a remarkable closing of international ranks against Saddam Hussein's aggression.

The President was also implying that there would be a quick and dazzling military victory, in the great tradition of American wars from at least 1846 to 1945. There would be a quick end to the Baghdad hostage crisis, erasing the memory of Tehran, and there would be a speedy reversal of aggression, erasing that of Vietnam. The armed forces would not have to 'fight with one hand tied behind their back', but would be allowed to do the job in their own way. Nor would there be a heavy toll of US lives, as there had been so disastrously in Vietnam and as the Iraqis had already declared there would be once again. More subtly, the President was even promising that there would be no attacks on enemy civilians that might revive memories of My Lai. This was to be a short and clean exercise in 'kicking butt', designed to bring satisfaction to all who had been frustrated by the Vietnam era.

These promises were very ambitious indeed, and at first sight even appeared contradictory. The renunciation of close political supervision over the military, for example, seemed to imply abdication from the higher task of winning hearts and minds worldwide. Conversely, the rigid rules of engagement placed upon the Air Force seemed to be *precisely* a case of tying its hands behind its back. What sort of liberty to choose its own fighting methods was left to a force that was not allowed either to suffer casualties or to cause collateral damage? How could one possibly hope to defeat 'the world's fourth largest army', especially when it had chemical weapons, without inevitably sending a sorry stream of body bags home to the States? How, finally, could one fight this particular war quickly and cleanly if the assassination of Saddam Hussein was officially disallowed?

To some extent these contradictions remained unresolved throughout the crisis. The very decision to launch Operation *Desert Storm* on 16th January 1991 was itself a case of politicians overriding their military advisers, since the ground forces had not been completely assembled by that date. Nor was it a good time for weather, since cloud cover during the first few days would lead to some frustrating delays in obtaining initial battle damage assessments – thereby allowing satirists to highlight the irony that a desert storm was holding up the operation that had been given precisely that name.

Political considerations also played an important part in determining the rules of engagement, and some of the twenty percent of air missions that were aborted would be attributed to strict observance of those restrictions. The urgent political need to hunt Scuds, once they started landing on Israel, further distorted the military

priorities of the air campaign. Again, it was the political desire to avoid allied casualties that helped prolong the air campaign far beyond the one- or two- day preliminary bombardment that had been seen in most earlier *blitzkrieg* campaigns. Many military commentators believed that the whole operation could have been finished in a single week, whereas in the event the political need for over-insurance meant it would take no less than six. Not only did this delay allow the Iraqis to intensify their persecution of the Kuwaitis, but it also gave them their chance to set fire to over 800 oil wells – a raging ecological disaster that would take many months to bring under control.

The lengthening of the air bombardment also surely led to an inevitable increase in unplanned 'collateral damage' to Iraqi civilians. When a Baghdad bunker containing hundreds of women

ABOVE

*Paulette White, a National Guard reservist from Alabama, sorting mail in Saudi Arabia. The regular delivery of mail to front line troops has long been recognized as an important element in maintaining military morale. In this war it would reach an unprecedented volume.*

RIGHT

*Air Force Sergeant Rory Horan of Arizona uses the efficient mail service to write home from his bunker in the desert.*

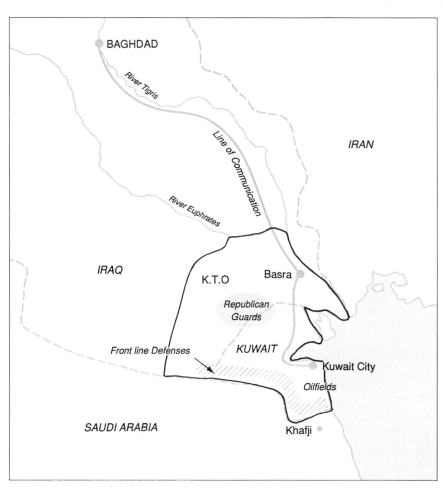

BAGHDAD

River Tigris

Line of Communication

IRAN

River Euphrates

IRAQ

K.T.O    Basra

Republican
Guards

Front line Defenses    KUWAIT

Kuwait City

Oilfields

SAUDI ARABIA    Khafji

**OPERATION DESERT SHIELD AND DESERT STORM
THE KUWAIT THEATER OF OPERATIONS**

and children was hit on 13th February, horrific scenes of carnage were instantly flashed around the world. The boast that precision munitions would avoid such atrocities was sadly undermined, especially since the bunker had been deliberately targeted in the belief that it was a military command post. This was not a rogue missile that had accidentally gone astray or been shot down before reaching its goal – which would have been bad enough as a technological embarrassment – but it turned out to have been two bombs aimed down the same line in quick succession, as the optimum way to penetrate that specific target. The incident was therefore doubly damaging; not only for its moral implications but also as an admission of defective target intelligence.

Despite all these problems, President Bush still succeeded in holding together his apparently inconsistent package of promises. One of the main reasons he could do this was that General

RIGHT

*The initial deployment was largely with air and naval forces, helping the bluff covering the later arrival of ground troops. Here a machine gunner on the command ship USS* La Salle *takes part in the United Nations blockade of Iraq.*

Schwarzkopf's astonishingly large arsenal of high-technology smart bombs and missiles really did, by and large, allow high value point targets to be hit without great collateral damage. Individual buildings and bridges in Baghdad could be crumpled in on themselves without neighboring blocks being affected – a clear advance over the Panama bombing only a year before. Even when Iraqi aircraft were hidden in concrete shelters, they could still be pursued and destroyed by pinpoint strikes. From its very first day, therefore, the war was successfully sold as a virtuoso demonstration and vindication of the new 'ET' weapons that had been so much discussed in the military literature of the previous fifteen years.

The new munitions allowed the air force's dream of self-sufficiency to come true at last. Within a few days of the start of Operation *Desert Storm* it had achieved complete air supremacy – the ability to operate anywhere in the skies over Iraq without significant interference from the enemy. Only 51 coalition aircraft were lost in the entire campaign, whereas the enemy's entire air force of some 700 planes was destroyed, trapped in its bunkers or forced to flee to neutral Iran. Air defence communications and radar installations were equally suppressed almost entirely, and after the first few days there ceased to be any firings of Iraqi SAMs.

Such a level of aerial victory was not in itself particularly new, since something comparable had been achieved over Germany and Japan in the closing days of WW2, or over Vietnam on a number of occasions in the 1960s and 1970s. In *Desert Storm*, however, the coalition air force was able to take one vital additional step that transformed an advantage into a decisive victory: it was able to use its total control of the air in order to achieve total control of the ground. In past campaigns the winning of air supremacy had rarely bestowed this ability, especially when the enemy had 'hunkered down' into fortified positions. In Vietnam, for example, the NVA had always been able to continue light infantry or guerrilla operations despite incessant bombing, while the VC's deep tunnel complexes were notoriously immune to air attack. Without precision munitions, the bombing planes had been forced to make repeated strikes in order to guarantee a kill: perhaps many hundred sorties to break a single bridge. But now, in 1991, a single strike involving no more than perhaps two or four sorties could usually destroy each target. With some 1,746 fixed wing aircraft available to the coalition, exclusive of many potent attack helicopters, between 1,500 and 3,000 sorties could be generated each day. This made for between 400 and 1,500 strikes per day, which proved to be a sufficient weight of firepower to destroy the enemy's army – almost exclusive of action by friendly ground forces.

The target list fell into four general categories, although they sometimes overlapped and competed with each other for priority. The first category included all the facilities connected with Iraq's ability to affect the air war: airfields, aircraft, air defense radars and ground to air weaponry. This list was soon effectively neutralized, as already detailed. The second category, potentially far more dangerous even than Saddam Hussein's air defenses, comprised his much-vaunted armory of unconventional weapons. These ranged from variants of the Scud ballistic missile, capable of hitting Israeli or Saudi cities, through chemical and biological weapon plants to nuclear reactors and even the rumored 'super gun'. Of these it was only the Scuds, and then only with conventional warheads, that would cause any damage – but the coalition bombing program still had to target all the other items on the lethal agenda. This led to the attack, for example, on a factory that the Iraqis claimed was making a baby milk formula, but that the coalition had identified as a probable producer of military gas. It was perfectly clear, at least, that Saddam Hussein could not be trusted in any way, since he did actually call for the use of chemical weapons in the last day of the ground war – although by then it was too late to put his order into effect.

Iraq's ability to continue firing Scuds throughout the war gave ample testimony to the robustness of that weapon, and the risks to be run if it had ever been married up to a more devastating warhead. The coalition's failure to destroy all the missiles on the ground, however, represented one of the few major holes in the 'ET' coverage of the battlefield. Surveillance was often too slow, or too much obstructed by cloud, or too easily deceived by enemy decoy tactics, for the missiles to be hit before firing. Nevertheless, the arrival of the lightning-fast Patriot close defence SAM usually allowed this hole to be plugged. Very few Scuds got through the Patriot defenses and only one caused heavy casualties – at Dhahran on 25th February, when 28 US service personnel, including two women, were killed in their barracks.

The third category of targets for the coalition air bombardment was what were rather loosely called 'command, control and economic facilities'. This was a catch-all title that included undoubted military communication centres such as ministry of defense buildings, microwave radio transmitters or field headquarters; but it also embraced much wider things such as Baghdad city's electricity supply, oil refineries, or Tigris bridges hundreds of miles from the fighting front. Although clearly designed in such a way as to

USS Tattnall *enters the Moslem world by passing through the Suez Canal on its way to Gulf duty, August 1990.*

*As war loomed closer, Saddam Hussein called up new categories of recruit for his army. Here the volunteer home defense People's Army drills in Baghdad, October 1990.*

minimize civilian casualties, the attack on this latter group of targets was widely interpreted as a direct assault on civilian morale and wealth. It was not designed to affect the ground battle in the KTO at all, as often claimed, but to cripple Iraq as a country and provoke a revolution. Both WW2 and Vietnam had shown how bombing tended to stiffen the spirit of resistance within a target population – yet here once again the strategists of air power appeared to be trying for precisely the same effect. At the very least it seemed a disproportionate use of resources, if a whole city had to be blacked out in order to stop a handful of generals talking to each other by radio.

The opposite side of this controversial coin was the question of assassinating Saddam Hussein himself. Since his régime rested almost entirely upon his personal reign of terror, the coalition had always been careful to state that it was fighting against him rather than against the Iraqi people. If he could be killed in his bunker with a single bomb, it would save everyone else a great deal of grief. Repeated attempts to do this were apparently made throughout the war, starting with an attack on his palace on the first night, and ending with a bunker strike during the last hours that was rumored to have killed many of his high command. Saddam Hussein nevertheless survived all assassination attempts, just as had Gaddafi in 1976. This meant that they could not become a viable alternative to the 'economic' attack on the civilian population after all, but merely a supplement to it – nor was their existence even acknowledged officially. Since the war was being fought to preserve the ground rules of international relations in the case of aggression between states, it was impossible to admit to breaking those ground rules in the case of assassinating foreign heads of state. Officially, therefore, a cruel process of strategic bombing had to be used to persuade the Iraqi people forcibly to change the régime themselves. After the ceasefire on 28th February this would lead to a bloody civil war rather than to a quick and clean transfer of power.

The fourth and final set of targets in the six week air war consisted of the Iraqi army within the KTO, and its immediate lines of communication. With some 4,200 tanks and 2,600 armored personnel carriers, this apparently formidable force outnumbered the coalition by around twenty percent. It also enjoyed the advantage of the defensive, being well dug in and covered by thick minefields and other obstacles. What it lacked, however, was any viable means of defense against air attack. For weeks it was subjected to carpet bombing by B-52s, and interdiction by the ubiquitous laser guided bombs against bridges or by roving fighter-bombers against supply convoys. Apaches and A-10s roved

far and wide, busting tanks and bunkers, while artillery pounded the front lines and coastal defenses.

The Iraqi army in the KTO was obviously doomed as soon as the coalition had won command of the air. This was proved dramatically between 30th January and 2nd February, when Saddam Hussein ordered a grand offensive in the area around the abandoned border town of Khafji. In the event he could move only the equivalent of a mechanized brigade into contact, and quickly saw it destroyed largely by air power. The small scale of the ground fighting for the allies can be gauged by the fact that less than 70 casualties were suffered, mainly among Saudi troops who mopped up residual snipers in the town after the 'battle' had died down.

Under any reasonable military calculation the Iraqis should have negotiated a withdrawal at that point; but they were not allowed to do so. Perhaps because he hoped to win long term credit among his political constituency, or perhaps because he believed in a miraculous repeat of the 1980s defensive victories over Iranian militias, Saddam Hussein insisted on holding out to the bitter end. The result was therefore inevitable. By 15th February the coalition was already claiming to have destroyed at least 1,300 tanks, 800 APCs and 1,100 artillery pieces. Although an estimation of 'body count' was studiously avoided by the briefers, this would suggest some 10,000 Iraqi casualties, quite apart from the carnage among soft skinned vehicles on the Kuwait-Basra road. The Iraqi army found it had no way of reading the

TOP

*In-flight refuelling made a vital contribution to the bombardment of Iraq, since many of the targets were over 500 miles from coalition bases. Here A-6 Intruders of Carrier Air Wing Three take on fuel from an Air Force KC-135.*

ABOVE

*Iraqi anti-aircraft fire lit up the sky over Baghdad "like the Fourth of July" according to eyewitnesses, on 16-17th January 1991, the night Operation Desert Storm began. Millions of rounds were fired at random, although the strike aircraft were often able to launch their precision weapons from miles outside the target area.*

battlefield, sustaining itself or even moving. Many of its front line troops were unwilling, over-age conscripts; starving, bewildered and only too ready to surrender as soon as they could be 'rescued' by the allied advance whenever it should come, and the sooner the better.

President Bush's demand for over-insurance and casualty-limitation would delay the unleashing of the main offensive until 24th February. The intervening time was spent intensifying the bombardment, refining intelligence – including that from special forces operating behind enemy lines – and setting up an elaborate deception plan. The latter involved naval action off the Kuwaiti coast suggestive of an amphibious landing, whereas in fact the 1st and 2nd Marine Divisions would be used entirely in a direct overland assault to Kuwait city, flanked by Arab contingents. Further inland a pattern of deployment and radio traffic was established to indicate that the main armored spearhead would drive close along the Kuwait-Iraq border straight towards Basra, whereas in reality it would be aimed much further around the Western flank. VII Corps, comprising 1st and 3rd Armored

Divisions, 1st Infantry Division and the British armor, would hook round behind the Republican Guard reserves and engage them from an unexpected direction. Meanwhile, 24th Mechanised, 101st and 82nd Airborne Division, together with the French Daguet Division, would sweep through the desert still further to the West, to establish themselves at Samawah and Nasiriyah, along the line of the Euphrates river. Since all bridges on the northward route out of the KTO through Basra would already be cut, these moves would complete an unbreakable encirclement of the entire KTO. A classic 'cauldron' would be established, from which the Iraqi army would find no escape apart from captivity.

Fortunately for the coalition, Saddam Hussein connived at the total destruction of his army by ordering its withdrawal from Kuwait at the very last minute. From his point of view he left it too late, since the trap had already been sprung before the movement could get fairly under way, so his withdrawal failed either to save the army or forestall the coalition's advance to the Euphrates. Instead, it merely helped stoke victims into the deadly traffic jam at the Mutlah gap on the road

back from Kuwait to Basra – the 'highway of death' – on which the retreating troops were mown down from the air in their thousands.

From the allied point of view, Iraqi withdrawal spelt a welcome last-minute reprieve from potentially very bloody house-to-house fighting through Kuwait city. The Marines were spared a second Hue, and the campaign degenerated into a military promenade that was as welcome to the beleaguered citizens of the emirate as it was to the Iraqi soldiers saving their own lives by surrendering *en masse*. Deep in the desert the

BELOW

*During the first three days of the attack, 40 percent of the precision targets were attacked by stealth fighters, which formed only 2 percent of the coalition air force. They fired smart munitions – an idea that had already been demonstrated in Vietnam, but never seen on such a scale as in Operation Desert Storm. Unannounced, these could descend from an apparently empty sky to land within a few inches of any chosen point, leading to the phrase being coined that "God is an armorer."*

armored advance was no less successful, and all but 200 of the enemy tanks were destroyed for negligible friendly loss. The 1st Armored Division, for example, accounted for more than two Republican Guard divisions, but lost only four tanks, two Bradleys and one helicopter. Total US casualties for the entire war amounted to just 79 killed, 213 wounded and 45 missing, with the combined allied forces losing approximately the same numbers. By contrast, Iraq lost its entire army killed, wounded, prisoner, missing or in mutiny against its own government.

The war to liberate Kuwait thus proved to be far less expensive in allied lives than the high command had predicted when it made sure almost ten percent of the in-country personnel comprised medical staff. The campaign was also far easier to win than many had expected, since even a six week aerial bombardment turned out to be longer than really necessary. The irony was perhaps that in Vietnam the US military establishment had confidently expected an easy victory with inadequate resources, whereas in the Gulf there had been much cautious talk but a completely overwhelming deployment of such resources.

RIGHT

*The Navy played a major part in the air war, just as it had in Vietnam. Here attack aircraft pack the flight deck of USS* Independence.

BELOW

*Preparing a Sidewinder AIM-7 missile for an F-15 fighter. A highly effective weapon for dog-fighting, this was one part of the US armory that was little used, since the enemy air force usually avoided combat – or flew to sanctuary in neighboring Iran.*

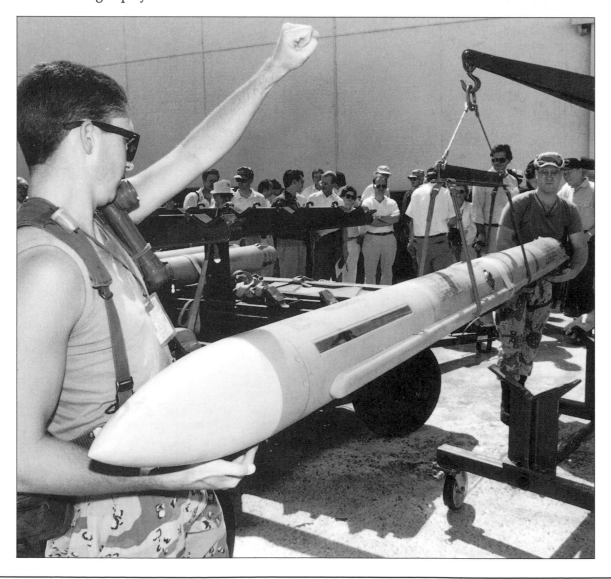

The 16-inch guns of the WW2-vintage battleship USS Wisconsin. Together with those of the battleship USS Missouri, these mighty rifles would conduct many fire missions against Silkworm missile batteries and other coastal targets. The battleships also fired Tomahawk cruise missiles deep into Iraq, including 196 in the 1st night of the war.

A-7E Corsairs from USS John F. Kennedy in training off the Saudi coast. This veteran aircraft is being phased out of service postwar, having made its first flight in 1965.

The "combat typist" enters a new era. Here a journalist files a report from Dhahran in a night when four Scud missiles were fired at the city – all of them intercepted by defending Patriot missiles.

Some of the first Iraqi prisoners taken in the war.
Twelve were taken from an oil platform being used
as an anti-aircraft site, on 19th January. By the end
of hostilities they would be joined by some 150,000
comrades in arms. Allied casualties, by contrast,
barely topped 150.

An anti-war march in Washington, D.C. on 19th
January. Many such protests were held throughout
the world as fighting continued, although the short
duration of this war meant they did not have time to
sway the mainstream of US public opinion.

ABOVE

Marines ride to the front at Khafji in "Hummers" –
successor to the classic Jeep. In this battle, fought
between 30th January and 2nd February, the Iraqis
made an assault with the equivalent of a mechanized
brigade, but it was soon destroyed with over 500
prisoners captured by coalition forces.

RIGHT

A column of the USMC's lightly-armored LAV-25
fighting vehicles. It was the close similarity in shape
between these vehicles and Iraq's Soviet-built BTR-
60s that led to a tragic accident during the Khafji
battle. Marines were killed in them by "friendly
fire" from US aircraft.

*The Apache anti-tank helicopter was called "the Mercedes of combat helicopters" for its high performance against Iraqi armor in the Gulf fighting. Costing $11 million per aircraft, with a further $30,000 for each of its Hellfire missiles, its efficacy had been questioned before the war – but no longer.*

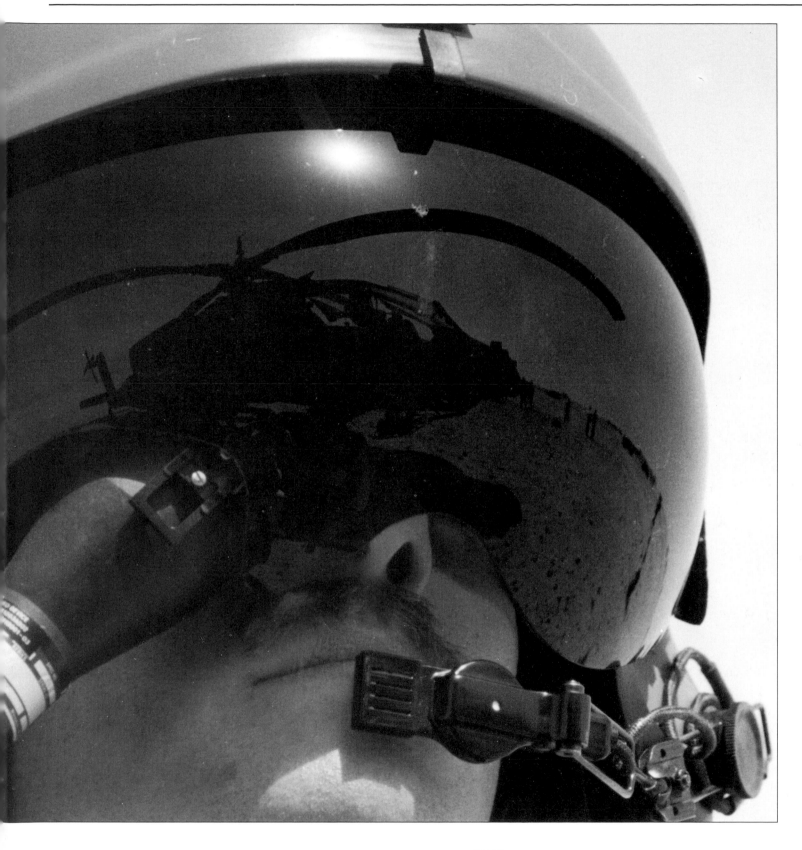

ABOVE

*An Apache is reflected in the high-tech visor of its
pilot as he prepares for a desert mission.*

ABOVE

*Soldiers of 1st ("Fighting Cav") Armored Division drive to the front in their Bradley infantry combat vehicle. This division would be credited with destroying some 630 tanks of the Iraqi Republican Guard in its outflanking drive to cut the road between Basra and Kuwait.*

**ABOVE**

*An MI-AI tank code-named "Death Chant" swings into action just before the final ground offensive.*

**LEFT**

*A soldier of the 82nd Airborne Division fires a Hummer-mounted TOW anti-tank missile in training. Fighting alongside the élite French Daguet Division, this fast-moving outfit made the widest-flanking move of all, and sliced though to Samawah on the Euphrates, just 150 miles from Baghdad itself.*